LET'S MAKE A CONTRACT

GETTING THROUGH UNHAPPY ROMANTIC RELATIONSHIPS

ANN SCHIEBERT, PsyD

Andrew Benzie Books
Walnut Creek, California

Published by Andrew Benzie Books
www.andrewbenziebooks.com

Printed in the United States of America

First Edition: July 2018

10 9 8 7 6 5 4 3 2 1

ISBN 978-1-941713-75-4

Book design by Andrew Benzie

Contents

Introduction

Did you ever get tired of dating people who just aren't or won't ever be a match for you? Have you spent time trying to rationalize why you have excused the unacceptable so often that it became acceptable? Have you developed a disappointing romantic relationship cycle in which you find yourself heartbroken more often than not? Me too!

I got lucky. It wasn't because I knew everything I wrote about in this book. I got lucky and met a person with a solid foundation and relationship skill set that certainly surpassed my own. I can't thank you enough, Tom Rohrer, PhD, for coming into my life and participating with me in making ours a healthy long-term romantic relationship. You bring daily joy, respect, kindness, and understanding. You are there when I need you and you seem to know when I need time alone. Thank you for being my rock star!

I also got lucky by having trusting patients who were courageous enough to try on new concepts and develop new behaviors that were not already in their relationship repertoire. In discussing their relationship disappointments, frustrations, and fears they opened the way for change. Many were able to move from acting on first romantic impulse to delayed gratification and the creation of deeper, more intimate relationships. Over time, more and more patients found long-lasting satisfaction from learning about limerence and by taking stock of their relationship behaviors and expectations. I was blessed with a formidable patient group who were fearless as they explored why they felt stuck in their own unhappy romantic relationships. Eventually, many of my patients ventured out of being stuck and tiptoed into a life filled with increased happiness and emotional stability.

It is my hope that each of you who have found yourself stuck in unsatisfying romantic relationships follows the guidelines provided on these pages. This book contains the answers that came to my patients through trial and error. Many of them have found lasting, joyful, satisfying relationships. If that is what *you* want, I hope this guide helps you in finding your heart's desire.

About This Book

Dear Readers:

Because I think it a little unusual, I want to share with you how the idea for this and the next book in the *Let's Make a Contract* series evolved.[1]

For years patients have come to me with a wide variety of situations they need help with: trauma, chemical dependency, relationship issues, anxiety, depression, emotion regulation, etc. One day while sitting in the chair in my office listening to a young woman share about an event that happened between her and her boyfriend, it occurred to me that at the root of much of the unhappiness I hear about in therapy sessions is relationships—unhappy relationships—especially unfortunate romantic relationships.

I considered just how many relationships each of us has! To name a few, we have relationships with our parents, siblings, other relatives, spouses, girlfriends/boyfriends, bosses, coworkers, friends, and even nonhuman entities like corporations. We even have a relationship with ourselves—a relationship commonly overlooked. As I returned my attention back to what my patient was saying I wondered, *how do we get ourselves into unhappy relationships and why on earth do we stay in situations that bring us emotional pain and suffering?*

After my patient had finished her time with me I gave this question deeper thought. I sat in my chair and conducted a somewhat superficial review of the many individuals who have sought therapeutic feedback from me. *What was the subject that was an issue for the majority of them? Was there a commonality?* I came up with a hypothesis. It appeared out of the blue and it was so simple that I immediately discarded it due to its being too uncomplicated. It seemed so obvious. It was devoid of fancy diagnostic descriptive words. It didn't contain any new idea that would render it an award. *Was it worthy of sharing?*

So here it is: We who find ourselves in unhappy relationships suffer because *we violate our own values* and, concurrently, we allow others to violate them also.

I noted the word "values." I had to define it. I looked it up in several dictionaries.

VALUES: THE REGARD THAT SOMETHING IS HELD TO DESERVE; THE IMPORTANCE OF SOMETHING; A PERSON'S PRINCIPLES OR STANDARDS OF BEHAVIOR; ONE'S JUDGMENT OF WHAT IS IMPORTANT IN LIFE.
—*Oxford English Dictionary*

---

[1] *The others are Getting Your Teen Through Substance Abuse (2016) and Getting Your Teen Through High School and Beyond (2016).*

I turned my thoughts back to past patients. How many of them were consciously aware of what their most important, uncompromisable values were?

The topic of values and how they relate to unhappiness in relationships has rarely come up in any of the therapy sessions I could remember. Yes, value violations were a main reason people came to therapy but the "problem" was not explored in terms of failures in honoring our values. The problem was defined more in terms of unfilled expectations on the part of the spouse, boyfriend, family, etc.

Presenting Problem	Expectation	Unnoticed Value Violation
S/he cheated on me.	Having only *me* as a partner.	Fidelity, honesty, respect.
My husband/ wife/ boyfriend/ girlfriend is drinking heavily. S/he's drunk a lot.	S/he will drink socially (often undefined).	Balance, moderation, responsibility.
I hate my job. My boss sucks.	To be treated fairly at work and guided in a respectful way.	Respect, cooperation.
My boyfriend disrespects me.	To be treated like an equal.	Respect, to be loved, compassion, cooperation, forgiveness.

Still sitting in my office chair, I reviewed my hypothesis: most of my patients' challenges in life were about unhappy relationships and their own inability to define and respect their most closely held values! How do they do this? How do people disrespect their values and how does that lead to unhappy relationships?

Here's the answer I came up with: when people notice a relationship issue that causes unhappiness, they have a tendency to rationalize, justify, or minimize it and explain it away. And all of these methods of trying to offset unhappiness accumulate into lies. The lie is "this is my lot in life and I can be somewhat happy in spite of the problem. Maybe the problem will resolve itself. After all, everybody has a problem or two." Another way of saying it is "I'm not really suffering. I'll get over it." It is the lies we tell ourselves that form the cement that keep us stuck in unhappy relationships. It is the lies that keep us in suffering mode. It is the lies that allow us to keep violating our own values.

"Wow!" I said to myself. That seems so harsh! We lie to ourselves about the suffering we go through! Really?

I thought about some current patients I was seeing (the names here are fictitious and the examples are a compilation of the challenges some of my current patients are facing):

Rhonda

Rhonda has been unhappily married for 15 years. She won't tell her husband she is unhappy because she fears conflict. Her husband gambles and continues to risk family finances. The presenting problem was that Rhonda lives in fear of "losing everything."

Rationalization: If my husband would only get some help then we'd be happy. It's not really that bad. I can cover his gambling debts. At least we own our home.

The Lie: I am OK because I have learned to live with this.

The Disrespected Value: Community expenditures must be agreed upon.

Sam

Sam has been with his boyfriend for three years. He loves his partner but feels taken advantage of because his partner works all the time and Sam has made himself in charge of taking care of their apartment as well as being a responsible employee in his own career. The presenting problem was that Sam feels "used" in his relationship.

Rationalization: My partner has a very important job and it is the least I could do to support his work by picking up our home.

The Lie: It's OK that I do much more to support our home environment than my partner does. It really doesn't bother me all that much.

The Disrespected Value: I believe that partners should divide community chores.

Adriana

Adriana is afraid of her mother, who repeatedly threatens to cut Adriana out of the will if she doesn't do whatever her mother wants her to do—such as grocery shopping, driving her to medical appointments, and coming over to her mother's assisted living facility to visit. The presenting problem was, how can Adriana talk herself into being "on call" to her mother?

Rationalization: My mom is lonely and she is more important than my three kids and their needs. After all, she has done so much for me, and she's old now.

The Lie: I owe my mother whatever she wants whenever she wants it.

The Disrespected Value: My kids are the most important thing in my life.

All these patients weren't saying their truth. It seemed that the formula for holding their unhappy relationship status quo was: feeling unhappy in a relationship leads to rationalization, justification, minimization, and denial, that is, the lie that keeps reinforcing the suffering and unhappiness in this relationship. The lie is without a solution, resolution, or reconstitution. The lie gives us covert permission to continue to violate our own values and to allow others to do the same.

Then this thought came to me: until you acknowledge that you are unhappy to yourself and to the person that you are in an unhappy relationship with, there will always be the lie between you. The lie will be a wedge and a barrier to a healthy, happy relationship.

I wondered, *Is this true in all relationships?* Remember that little-recognized relationship noted in the beginning of this introduction, the one about the relationship you have with yourself? I can't think of any situation in which lying to ourselves about our unhappiness in a business, romantic, family, or any other type of relationship would be a benefit. Lies about value violations cause us internal discordance. Maybe we don't tell our bosses that we are unhappy in our business relationship with them, but to not admit it to ourselves is a self-inflicted value insult.

I got up from my office chair and took a walk outside while I considered if I should impart these ideas so that my readers could use them as a guideline with which to reconceptualize the cause of their unhappy relationships: value violations.

As I churned this question around, I noticed a couple sitting on a park bench. They appeared to be arguing. I sat down on a bench near them and (I admit it) eavesdropped on their quarrel. Here's what I heard:

FEMALE: You are so mean to my kids. I want you to treat them with respect. You can't call them names. Every time you do, I feel awful.
MALE: There's no harm in name calling. My dad did that to me. Look at me! I grew up fine! I hold a good job. Your kids are wusses. They need to toughen up.
FEMALE: Please try to change that? Please?
MALE: Whatever. OK. I'll try.

There it was. The female in this relationship was allowing her boyfriend to disrespect her children. They had two different values about name calling and belittling children. But the female didn't address *her* unhappiness in this relationship. She focused on the presenting problem—name calling. She didn't say, "I want you to know, I am unhappy in our relationship because you call my kids names." Why didn't she? I certainly don't know, but I could make an educated guess that she didn't want to lose the relationship so she "sacrificed" her values to the unhappy relationship she was in.

Readers, you might say, "Yeah, but what if all the rest of the relationship was good?" I would ask you if allowing someone to belittle your children could ever be offset by any "good" components of a relationship? If this woman's uncompromisable value is being kind to her children, then all the rest of the relationship is negatively tinged by the value violation.

In an attempt to not be identified as a nosy eavesdropper, I got up from my perch on the bench and walked around the duck pond in the middle of the park. I asked myself, *What can people do to understand and respect their own values and search for situations in which their standards are respected? What can people do to stop perpetuating unhappy relationships?*

As I continued my trek around the pond, I reconsidered the various types of relationship problems I have seen over the many years I have been a psychologist. It occurred to me that patients fit into two categories: those who had unhappy romantic relationships and those who were in unhappy relationships with parents, bosses, elderly parents, etc. While all unhappy relationships have some things in common, it's the unhappy romantic relationships that elicit the most fear when it comes to making changes or respecting our own values. Unhappy romantic relationships (URRs) bring with them a cargo of luggage full of functionally obsolete beliefs, painful emotions, denial, euphoric recall, feelings of hopelessness, and being stuck. For those reasons, the subject of unhappy romantic relationships deserves a discourse separate from other types of relationships.

I must suppose that if you are reading this, you have some experience with URRs. I imagine you are reading this because you seek information that will help you alleviate your suffering. Or, you are reading this in hopes that it will provide you with enlightenment about how to select partners in the future so that when you enter into a new relationship it will be more healthy and happy than those you have had in the past. This book has three goals:

1. To provide you with a unique way of examining how you get yourself into, and why you have stayed in romantic relationships that are unkind, unloving, not satisfying, and not supportive.

2. To facilitate you in articulating the values that you repeatedly violate in your romantic relationships. It is those value violations that have led to past suffering in your URRs.

3. To help you create new pathways that will lead you to finding a happy and healthy romantic relationship in which you and your partner share common values.

How to Use This Book

This book is not about providing readers with a new way to create negative self-judgments. Many of us have PhDs in that area. It is not meant to help you take a "look at how I've screwed up" inventory. It is intended to provide you with a different compass with which to look at how you have made decisions that have led to URRs in the past.

My goal is to offer a guide with which we can investigate how we "screen" potential romantic relationships, why we often rush into new romances, and why we stay in relationships that cause us suffering. I hope it also provides ideas for how one can leave unhappy romantic relationships with grace, peace, and emotional finality.

Once you have examined what has happened in the past, you can cast your eyes toward a happier tomorrow and focus on new ways to select people who are a match. You can learn how to screen for common values based on our *uncompromisable* ones.

Use this book as a vehicle for hope: hope that once you learn to respect your values you will then be able to screen for romantic relationships that will honor your ethics, principles, and standards. Remember, if *you* don't know what your values are, who will? And if *you* don't know what your values are, the only way you will know they have been violated is when you start to suffer in what becomes an unhappy romantic relationship.

Do the Worksheets.

Do the Value Sort.

Write down *your* uncompromisable values.

Tell yourself the truth.

Make contracts with yourself and others (the templates are provided).

Respect your contracts.

Remember
- **RR** means Romantic Relationship.
- **PRR** means Potential Romantic Relationship.
- **URR** means Unhappy Romantic Relationship.
- **HRR** means Happy Romantic Relationship—what we all strive to have.

(The next book in the series will address difficult *nonromantic* relationships.)

Thank you for reading this. It was written with the intent of facilitating you to empower yourself to be steadfast to your values in a romantic relationship that brings happiness instead of emotional distress!

NOTE: All contracts in this book are available in electronic form to download, modify, and print. See page 212 for more information.

CHAPTER 1

The Rush to Romance

What is this? Let's start with some stories. The theme of the story is one that we see on TV, hear from our teens and our friends. The story is told in the Cinderella fairytale, *Tangled*, *Pretty Woman*, and the movie *Ever After* with Drew Barrymore. It goes like this: guy meets girl or girl meets guy and after getting through some obstacles they fall in all-consuming love and presumably live happily ever after. We don't get to see how the story plays out three years later. We only get to see the meeting and the "dream of true love" come true. Usually there is some type of challenge or struggle between the beginning and the end. The dream is actualized in the length of the movie or in the time it takes to read the fairytale. After years of counseling adolescents, young adults, couples, and parents, I have come to realize that much of the foundation of American "love" and relationships rests on the many fairytales that we watch on TV or see in the movies.

Ben and Carlie

Ben met Carlie in college. In their freshman year they were each other's first sexual experience.

Ben announced to his relatives, "I love Carlie so much! We've been through so much together! We are going to marry! I know she's the one! Plus, I am so attracted to her whenever I see her."

Ben didn't say, "I loathe that Carlie smokes weed, that she parties all the time, and she is a total slob in the apartment we share."

Ben thought, *Carlie will change. She has a hard past to overcome and we can make it together. I can overlook the things that bother me.*

Carlie broadcast to her family, "I am going to marry Ben. He is so supportive. I need him. He organizes me. He fills in my empty spaces."

Carlie didn't say, "Ben is such a nag and a drag. Plus he is a neatnik—I hate that about him. He's so rigid. Everything has to be in its place."

Carlie thought, *Ben will just have to get over it. He will. I just know he will loosen up. He needs to smoke some pot.*

And they marched down the aisle, said "I do," and *did not* live happily ever after.

Sarah and Rock

Rock was the handsomest guy his high school had ever seen. He had made the varsity football team. He was a great student. He was popular. He was elected to be president of the junior class. Rock had it all going on. He planned on attending college, joining a fraternity, and having a good time. Rock saw himself as "a kewl dude; friend to all."

Sarah was intelligent, funny, a cheerleader, and popular. She wanted to go to college, join a sorority, and be a nurse. But Sarah didn't see herself as she was. She thought she was overweight, too short, and not attractive to the high school guys.

One day Sarah's friend Nancy told her that one of Rock's friends had inquired if Sarah had a boyfriend. Nancy said that Rock was the one who wanted to find out. Sarah couldn't believe it! "Me?" she said to Nancy. "What would Rock ever see in me?"

Being a great friend, Nancy told Sarah, "Why not you? You are great! Rock should be so lucky." Sarah didn't believe it.

One night Rock unexpectedly texted Sarah and asked her to meet him at the gym after school. Sarah counted the minutes. After what seemed like an eternity, there they were, in the gym, face to face. Rock told Sarah he liked the way she cheered. She told Rock she loved watching him play football. Sarah flushed. Her heart beat faster. Rock walked her home and held her hand.

Rock thought, *I wonder how I'll do in tomorrow's game? I really need to do my homework when I get home.*

Sarah thought, *I hope he asks me out. I wish we would go steady. Should I ask him out? I wonder if we start going together if we should go to the same university.*

Rock got home, shot some hoops with his brother, did his homework, ate dinner, watched TV, and went to sleep.

Sarah got home, and checked her phone all night hoping that Rock would text her. She called Nancy to ask if she thought she should text Rock. They had an hour-long conversation about Rock. Sarah didn't do her homework. She could hardly eat dinner. She went to bed, dreaming of Rock.

Sarah hadn't noticed that all Rock talked about was himself and sports. He hadn't asked her one question about herself.

Rock didn't notice that Sarah blew bubbles and cracked her gum during the entire walk. Gum chewing was one of his pet peeves.

Welcome to infatuation, whose formal name is *limerence*. It is how many relationships begin. It is the reason that many relationships end.

Before we start examining the sequence of "love," we want to be sure we understand the initial and normal phenomena of attraction that is stimulated by a natural hormonal-biochemical urge to bind with another person. Remember, everyone's brain is designed to promote his/her genes and all sexual and romantic attraction begins with a "chemical love" that is powered by oxytocin, phenylethylamine, dopamine, and norepinephrine. In a very simplified way, let's examine these transmitter grenades that lead humans to both healthy and unhealthy "love."

Oxytocin: known as the "cuddle chemical" or the "love hormone," it helps increase our sensitivity toward other people. Oxytocin has been compared to the drug ecstasy (MDMA) in that it induces strong feelings of trust, empathy, and compassion.

Phenylethylamine (PEA): a natural amphetamine that delivers to us that feeling of being on top of the world; that euphoric feeling of being "high." It is the chemical that fuels our ability to stay up all night obsessing about the object of our affection. PEA clouds good judgment, distorts thinking, and increases reactivity and impulsivity.

Dopamine: the lust, adultery, motivation, and addiction neurotransmitter that is the biggest seeker of rewards of them all. It provides the "high."

Norepinephrine: produces the racing heart and feelings of excitement.

Once this hormonal and biochemical "love cocktail" takes effect, limerence enters the mix.

Genuine Romantic Love

It is necessary to understand "real love" so we can see the differences between the healthy and unhealthy categories. The word "love" is used in so many contexts that for the purposes of this book, we are using the words "genuine love" or "real love" to refer to a *healthy* type of romantic connection. "Real love" comes with a secure bond; nothing outside the relationship or any subject being discussed (school, work, kids, etc.) is more important than the relationship itself. Impediments to the relationship are overcome by one's dedication to it. According to Marshall B. Rosenberg's *Nonviolent Communication: A Language of Compassion*, the genuine kind of romantic love comes with a physical bond, a balanced sense of shared identity, and a psychological and emotional reciprocity.

Much research has found that "real" love starts with a meeting and, over time, evolves into liking and a friendship that is able to withstand the test of life's trials. In "real love" the chemically induced attraction does not provide the foundation of the relationship... but it certainly does provide the beginning of one.

Note that with "genuine" love, intimacy often comes *after* the liking and friendship. Real and healthy love includes equality, honesty, respect, independence, and humor. It provides comfort for both parties, and offers enduring enjoyment of everyday experiences. There is a mutual agreement of monogamy and a track record of loyalty and devotion.

Ben and Fred

Ben met Fred in college. They both came out in their freshman year. They were roommates in their college dorm and, as such, had time to discuss their fears about coming out, their thoughts about possible family reactions, and planning the timing of each of their announcements to their parents. They formed a support system that was mutual, and based on honesty and common experiences.

Ben and Fred found out that going to sporting events, eating out, and playing guitar together with a new band Fred had formed was great fun.

Ben hated that Fred smoked marijuana. He hated the smell and how Fred acted when he was high. One day Ben told Fred how much he disliked his friend's habit. Fred invited Ben to try some weed. Ben declined. They had a conversation about how much they enjoyed each other's company. Ben told Fred that he really liked to be with him when he wasn't high. Fred told Ben he smoked pot to avoid thinking about some of his family history and to get to sleep. Ben supported Fred in getting some therapy. Fred did.

Over time, Ben and Fred discovered they had passion for each other and became intimate. They decided to be in a committed relationship and to rent an apartment together. Before apartment hunting, Fred told Ben that his "neatnik living style" irritated him. They discussed the problem and decided to rent a two-bedroom apartment so Fred would have a room he could keep in any condition he wanted. Fred agreed to keep the community areas clean and uncluttered.

They moved in together. They went through the usual adjustment period that challenges every committed partnership. They developed a relationship based on mutual love and respect. They helped each other complete college. They worked through problems together. They found emotionally rewarding jobs. They married. They relish their individuality and their relationship. So far, they've been together ten years.

Limerence

Limerence, a "crush," looks like love, feels like love—*but it is* not *love!*

Limerence is like the sonic force that fuels a drama. It is infatuation that is contingent on sexual attraction. Limerence is accompanied by the expectation that one's feelings for someone (usually a person whom we don't know very well) will be reciprocated. It involves obsessive thoughts, intrusive thinking, fantasies, compulsory longing, and emotional attachment for another person. The end goal of limerence is to join—form a pair—*fast!* (All attractions can start this way but for "real love" these transient feelings are NOT the basis of the relationship.)

Limerence picks us up like the tornado did with Dorothy in *The Wizard of Oz*. Instead of landing in Munchkinland, we find ourselves lost in unreasoned passion and separated from our balance and good judgment. Limerence can envelop us in such a sense of euphoria that we lose our ability to make rational decisions. We become overpowered and our balance is altered by longing for reciprocation and fear of rejection. Limerence is much like an addiction to another person. That other person and our urgency for "coupling," becomes the organizing principle of our decisions in all areas of our life.

How do we know we are in a state of limerence? We tremble, experience heart palpitations, awkwardness, loss of appetite, insomnia, shyness, and confusion. (While it is true that many healthy relationships start this way, with the limerent relationship these feelings exclusively form the foundation of bonding.)

While in a state of limerence, one's emotions can span from intense joy to extreme despair; these depend on one's perception of whether or not the object of our desire (the *limerent*) feels the way we do. Metaphorically speaking, limerence comes with a pair of "rose-colored glasses" because it provides a shield that disallows us from seeing the person to whom we are attracted as they really are. When signs of desire are reciprocated, one's ability to be clear-sighted flies out the window.

Limerence is fueled by the "love cocktail" that endures between six months and two years. Limerence itself exerts its power between three and five years at a maximum. This chemical and emotional combination lasts just long enough to bear children. They are the ones who pay the price for a limerent partnership.

When the "cocktail" begins to wear off we often remain in the relationship, wondering where the euphoria went. After all, that high provided the cement to the relationship. As we gradually become aware of the faults of our loved one, we are stymied as to why the "love of our life" has changed. *Why can't they be the way they used to be? They were kind, loving, attentive, and thoughtful. They talked with us on the phone all night. We texted a thousand times a day. How did that fun and adventurous person turn into a negative, critical, inattentive slob who doesn't lift a finger to contribute to the relationship?* We nag, lecture, cry, get angry, and try every way we can think of to rekindle the relationship with that person we couldn't get enough of. We become heartbroken and expend more and more energy trying to "make" our loved one "see the light" and change back into the person we initially saw at the beginning of the relationship—but they won't do it! They won't revert back. We wear ourselves out.

It is usually a scary and sad time when we begin to believe that the person we "got" isn't the person we thought he/she was. We feel frantic. We call our friends. We give examples of how our loved one's behavior has changed—we make a case for our unhappiness (which is based on the behavior of our mate).

Infatuation and heartbrokenness does not come with a secure bond. Limerence has often been described as "love at first sight." It is at the unhealthy end of the love spectrum. With the dilution of the "love cocktail" and the offing of one's rose-colored glasses, the relationship usually dies. The end of limerence is one of the main reasons for the end of relationships.

Let's summarize the differences between love and limerence. In Dr. Gilda Carle's article "Is It Love… or Limerence?" she offers seven ways to distinguish them.[2]

---

[2] *www.match.com/magazine/article/12710/Is-It-Love-Or-Limerence.*

Love

- supports your personal happiness and sets the stage for you to connect with someone who is also able and wanting to connect.

- means give-and-take between two people.

- consists of a healthy nonattachment wherein two people pursue their own interests and then reunite to share their experiences with each other. Nonattachment does not mean not caring. Rather, it connotes that parties in a caring relationship have the freedom to enjoy their individuality.

- means honest communication between two people.

- involves flexible gender roles that may be contrary to male and female stereotypes. For example, in a heterosexual relationship, the male may vacuum and wash the dishes while the female could wash the cars and keep the garage clean.

- is a true partnership in which each person supports the other.

- involves healthy sexual closeness and physical intimacy with your partner.

Limerence

- seeks control over your partner in an attempt to make this person dependent on you.

- involves an unrequited infatuation by just one individual. When those feelings are not returned, obsession, sometimes self-destructive behavior, and feelings of being "insanely mad" can take over.

- exhibits an overwhelming sense of "attachment," which can feel like a dependency that often serves to smother the other party.

- involves game-playing and manipulation. These are unreliable means of securing love.

- endorses the antiquated roles of feeble, swooning women and aggressive, macho men.

- positions someone to become a crush's savior. The aim is to become the hero or heroine for which the limerent object will be eternally grateful, and then grant that partner the ultimate reward of sticking around afterward.

- omits any sexual fantasies because its prime goal is to attract the limerent object's attention, obligation, and devotion.

How Can Limerence Affect Relationships?

There is very little research on this topic but perhaps by looking at statistics, we can draw some tentative conclusions.

Getting Engaged

How Long Do Couples Date Before Getting Engaged?[3]

Timeframe	Percentage	Cumulative %
< 6 Months	8%	8%
6 Months to 1 Year	18%	26%
1 to 2 Years	20%	46%
2 to 3 Years	16%	62%
3 to 4 Years	12%	74%
4 to 5 Years	10%	84%
5 to 6 Years	5%	89%
6 to 7 Years	5%	94%
7 to 8 Years	2%	96%
8 to 9 Years	1%	97%
9 to 10 Years	1%	98%
> 10 Years	2%	100%

According to the data, a whopping 74% of people get engaged within the first four years of knowing each other. Of that 74%, 8% get engaged at six months or earlier and 18% get engaged in one year. This suggests that most people are getting engaged well within the period when the "love cocktail" and limerence could be influences.

---

[3] *www.weddingtonway.com/wedding-guide/style/wedding-dresses-and-bridal-gowns/will-you-get-engaged-this-valentines-day.*

Dating

Time Spent Dating Before Proposal[4]

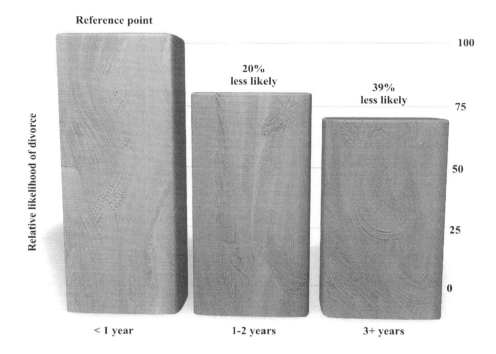

Research suggests that the percentages of staying together increase with the time one waits to get engaged/married. The longer people date, the less likely it is that they divorce and the less likely that the "love cocktail" and limerence will be the foundational factor in the relationship.

Living Together

A current popular phenomenon that we must also consider is that many people are living together before they marry. Most often the thinking around cohabitation (in my language) is that living together will bypass the "love cocktail" and limerence effect. "We will really get to know each other." "We're not ready to get married—let's live together and see what happens." However, research indicates that those who lived together before they married had a 33% higher rate of divorce than those

---

[4] *Olga Khazan, "Divorce Proof Marriage," The Atlantic (October 14, 2014).*

who waited to marry before they lived together,[5] and those who lived together or married at age 18 saw a 60% rate of divorce![6]

These statistics suggest a large rate of incompatibility. Many couples ignore signs that they aren't "meant for each other" and marry anyway. Why? Again, research finds that this is because of what Dr. Scott Stanley calls "The Inertia Effect": they slide into marriage without the discussion about sharing an entire life together and they also avoid the inconvenience of ending the relationship.[7] They slide into marriage even if their relationship was not a happy one. Many have reported telling themselves, *marriage will make our relationship better* or *marriage and a baby will make this relationship better*. My contention is that the "love cocktail" and limerence led them to try to solidify a relationship that was not based on a foundation that leads to a successful union.

Here are some facts about cohabitation:[8]

1. The greatest rates of cohabitation are among high school graduates.
2. Only a little more than half of couples who first cohabited ever get married.
3. Couples who live together are at a greater risk for divorce than noncohabiting couples.
4. Cohabiting couples are almost eight times more likely to separate due to discord than married couples in the first year of a relationship.
5. Cohabitating couples had a separation rate of five times that of married couples.
6. Cohabiting couples are twice as likely to experience infidelity in the first year of their relationship than are married couples.
7. Noncohabiting couples have a 20% chance of being divorced within five years. If a couple lived together before marriage, that statistic jumps to 49%.
8. Couples who cohabit have higher levels of depression and substance abuse than their married cohorts.

---

[5] *Lauren Fox, "The Science of Cohabitation: A Step Toward Marriage, Not a Rebellion," The Atlantic (March 20, 2014).*

[6] *Arielle Kuperberg, "Age at Coresidence, Premarital Cohabitation, and Marriage Dissolution: 1985–2009," Journal of Marriage and Family (April 2014).*

[7] *Scott M. Stanley, "Sliding vs. Deciding: The Hidden Risk of Cohabitation," Psychology Today blog (July 29, 2014).*

[8] *Sheri Stritof, "Cohabitation Facts and Statistics You Need to Know," The Spruce (April 13, 2017), https://www.thespruce.com/cohabitation-facts-and-statistics-2302236; Jodee Redmond, "Divorce Statistics and Living Together Before Marriage," Love to Know, http://divorce.lovetoknow.com/Divorce_Statistics_and_Living_Together; "Divorce Statistics - Divorce Rates," U.S.A.L.S., http://www.usattorneylegalservices.com/divorce-statistics.html.*

Union Dissolution Within Five Years of
Birth of First Child in 20- to 29-Year-Old Mothers[9]

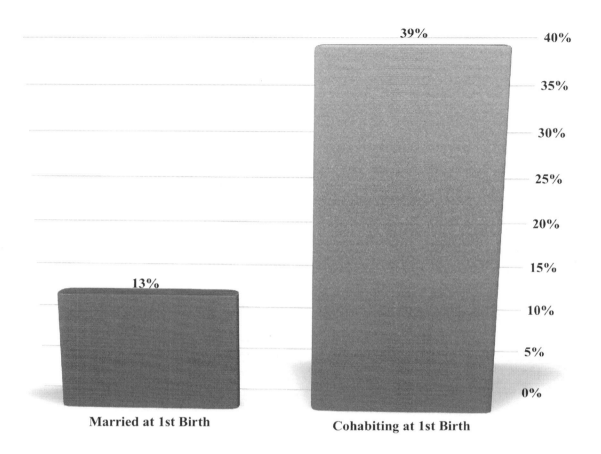

[9] OECD (Organisation for Economic Co-operation and Development) database,
www.oecd.org/els/soc/SF_2_3_Age_mothers_childbirth.pdf.

Divorce

So far, we have looked at how the "love cocktail" and limerence may have influenced dating, engagements, and cohabitation. Now let's look at divorce. (Note: Break-ups from cohabitating relationships are not included in the statistical divorce rates.)

Divorce Rates Table from the National Center for Health Statistics of the CDC[10]

Year	Divorces & Annulments	Population	Rate per 1,000 Total Population
2014	813,862	256,483,624	3.2
2013	832,157	254,408,815	3.3
2012	851,000	248,041,986	3.4
2011	877,000	246,273,366	3.6
2010	872,000	244,122,529	3.6
2009	840,000	242,610,561	3.5
2008	844,000	240,545,163	3.5
2007	856,000	238,352,850	3.6
2006	872,000	236,094,277	3.7
2005	847,000	233,495,163	3.6
2004	879,000	236,402,656	3.7
2003	927,000	243,902,090	3.8
2002	955,000	243,108,303	3.9
2001	940,000	236,416,762	4.0
2000	944,000	233,550,143	4.0

As we can see, about half of US marriages end in divorce. According to the American Psychological Association, the average age for couples going through their first divorce is 30. From this information, it might be wise to date longer and marry after age 30.

Consider the rates of divorce within the first five years of marriage and the main reported reasons for marital dissolution:

---

[10] *www.cdc.gov/nchs/nvss/marriage_divorce_tables.htm.*

Divorce Rates Within the First Five Years of Marriage[11]

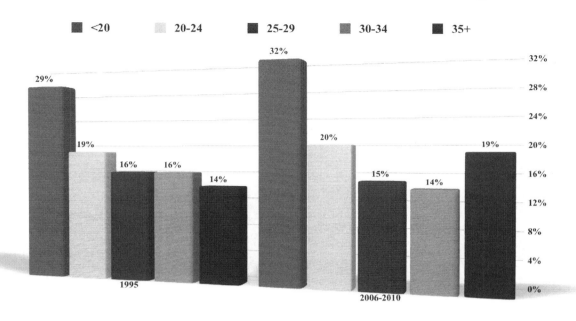

Most Frequently Cited Reasons for Divorce[12]

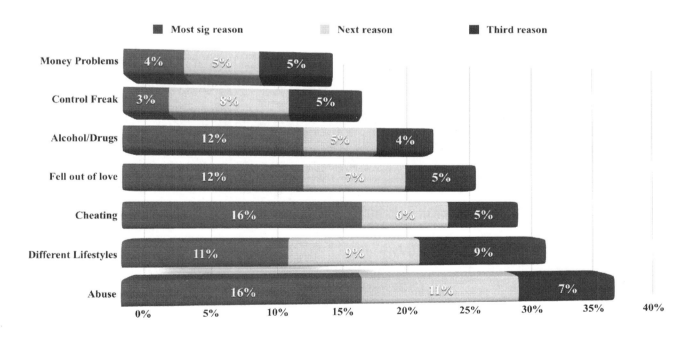

---

[11] *Institute for Family Studies, https://ifstudies.org/blog/want-to-avoid-divorce-wait-to-get-married-but-not-too-long.*

[12] *https://www.quora.com/What-was-the-biggest-single-reason-that-people-divorce.*

How might we interrupt these statistics? If we knew our "partner" better, don't you think we would have realized the money-spending habits, control issues, addiction problems, lifestyle differences, and abusive tendencies before we made our commitment legal? If our rose-colored glasses were off, don't you think that these relationship obstacles would have given us cause for a pause?

There is no known statistical study on relationship dissolution rates affected by the "love cocktail" and limerence that this writer could find. In the absence of numerical documentation, sometimes we have to draw conclusions based on other statistical evidence. From the statistics offered here, perhaps we could conclude that chemicals combined with limerence are a factor in our relationship culture. If this is an accurate assumption, we are not basing our relationships on a healthy foundation.

So just why do we rush into relationships/engagements/marriages? Other than the limerence and "love chemical" reasons, what could possibly motivate us?

Rushing into Relationships

Here are the top 11 reasons people rush into relationships—usually during the time when the "love cocktail" and "limerence" are in control:

1. Sex—we may be having sex even before a relationship begins. Many of us are thinking that if we are in a relationship *after* sex, we get to know the person.
2. The primal desire to bond with someone we "love" and who "loves" us. We want to belong.
3. Fear—fear of being alone, of having one's biological clock run out, of not finding the "right one," of never having the fantasy dream wedding, of being the last single person in your group of friends, and the list goes on and on.
4. Believing "a relationship will complete me."
5. Believing a relationship gives definition to our life.
6. External pressures: your relatives just *love* the person you brought to meet them.
7. Pregnancy—you have sex and now you find yourself with a child on the way.
8. "Feels like home." The dynamic with the person in your life feels like your family of origin. It feels "comfortable" even if it is unhealthy.
9. Codependency—you consciously or unconsciously take on new "projects" to "fix," "rescue," "save," give advice to, and lecture about why they need to change.
10. A new relationship diverts us from our problems.
11. Sex/relationship addiction.

Let's examine these 11 reasons people rush into a relationship.

Sex

For many, having sex is equated with being in a relationship. It is important to remind oneself that "sex" and "relationship" are actually two different things. Sex involves intimate physical activity and is usually related to sexual intercourse. A romantic relationship involves emotions (and sex) as well as a commitment to the bond between two people… and so much more. (See "Healthy Romantic Relationships," Chapter 6.) So many of my patients are devastated that they have sex with someone and never hear from them again, or think that if they had not been the pursuer, there would not have been further communication.

Nathan and Tina

Meet Tina, an attractive 16-year-old who is from an emotionally detached family. Tina feels empty. She wants love.

Nathan, a 17-year-old football player at Tina's high school, just broke up with his girlfriend of two months. He asks Tina out for coffee. They meet at a local coffeehouse and spend two hours processing Nathan's split-up. Then they go to Nathan's car, drive to a location notorious for "car sex," and after making out, have sex. Nathan takes Tina back to the coffeehouse. Tina gets in her car and drives home.

Then the texting, emailing, and phone calls begin. Tina wants a "relationship." Nathan just wanted to salve his residual dejected feelings from his ex breaking up with him.

Tina pursues. She and Nathan meet to have sex.

The sexual dynamic in a relationship must be cultivated. If it is, sex becomes only a part of the relationship, and for healthy relationships sex is not the principal organizing factor.

The Primal Desire to Bond

Perhaps the idea of belonging is the opposite of the concept of being lonely. Being loved and part of someone else's life is important to many of us, but let's look at "being part of someone else's life" more closely. What does that mean? Often we walk into someone's life without even knowing what that life is all about!

Stan and Lindsey

Let's briefly look at 28-year-old Lindsey. She met Stan at a bar. They drank too much, went to Stan's apartment, had sex and "have been together ever since because we fell in love immediately." After four years together, Lindsey began to evaluate what she had signed up for: while Stan had a good job and at times was very entertaining, he came from an alcoholic family that was fraught with arguing, disrespect, occasional domestic violence, and siblings who had difficulties with job retention due to their uncontrolled emotional reactions to authority. Stan's role in his family was that of peacemaker, so every family problem landed at Stan's feet for him to mediate. Almost every night, Stan's cell phone would ring with a family issue for him to solve.

Lindsey came from a family in which alcohol had never been an issue, and she and her sister had successful careers and got along well. Her family didn't have drama and trauma as a regular occurrence.

She became exhausted by the nightly phone calls. She and Stan argued over her view of them as an invasion of their time together, and she labeled Stan's need to "be there for his family when they need me" as an addiction. Lindsey felt that he put his family's problems before their relationship.

Lindsey became detached from Stan. Then she became pregnant. She fantasized that their baby would bring them closer together; it drove them further apart. The nightly phone calls did not stop, the new parents were sleep deprived, and Lindsey would not let Stan's family be alone with the baby. Stan became infuriated.

This relationship was seeded in Lindsey's need to "belong." But she didn't investigate further. Lindsey would have greatly benefitted if she had asked herself the question, *Belong to* what*? I want to belong to* what*?* Defining what the "what" is can lead us to clearer decision-making.

Fear

Conscious and unconscious fear can be huge motivating factors that lead us into relationships. Let's look at some of these fears.

Fear of Being Alone

From the many years of unscientific polls I have conducted with patients, fear of being alone was the number two reason people rushed into relationships. When someone tells me they are in a relationship because they fear being alone, I always follow up with the question, "Fear of what?" The usual response is, "Hmm, I don't know." With guided exploration, people often discover that they fear "not having a body at home with me at night; not having someone to come home to." This has held true even when people are in abusive relationships because they cling to the hope that things will change. They are addicted to hope.

When we think about "lonely," we have to define what "lonely" means to us. Does it mean that we stay in a relationship no matter how we are treated just so we will have someone home with us at night? Does being "alone" mean isolating in one's house? Does it mean we'll settle for any person who comes along? It is important that if you are controlled by the fear of being alone *you* do the work necessary to define exactly what that concept means to you. Otherwise we hold ourselves hostage to a fear that we can't describe.

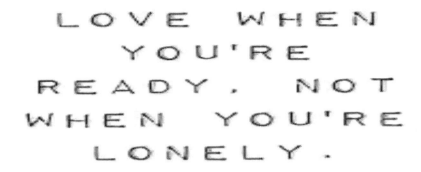

Fear of being alone is also known as *autophobia*.

Fear of My Biological Clock Running Out

So many women "settle" for a committed relationship/marriage because they want to have a family. Often they don't take the time to assess what parenting skills they or their mate actually have.

Jennifer and Craig

Jennifer, 32, met Craig, 28, and there was an "instant attraction." They dated, did activities together, met each other's families, and had fantastic sex. Jennifer just knew that Craig would be the perfect dad.

However, in making this decision, Jennifer had overlooked that Craig had a rage problem. He threw his golf clubs when he didn't make the putt. He banged the ping-pong paddle on the table when he lost the game. He slammed his beer down when his favorite team lost. Jennifer told herself that it was just with sports that Craig acted this way. Then she noticed that during disagreements, Craig would slam doors and yell to get his point across. After six months of dating, Craig proposed. Three months later they were married, and nine months later little Stacy was born. Jennifer had satisfied her need to have a family.

But was it the family she had dreamed about? Absolutely not! What Jennifer had dreamed about was that Craig would be a kind and gentle dad. But Craig got angry when the baby woke him up or when he couldn't make the baby stop crying. He got angry when the baby spread pureed food all over her face and high chair. The baby began to cry when Craig was around. Jennifer kept hoping things would change. By the time her little one was three years old, Jennifer divorced Craig because of his anger issues.

It is not easy to forecast how someone will parent. Perhaps we would benefit from paying less attention to our biological clock and more attention to giving ourselves time to figure out what we want in a partner, and if those criteria also meet the benchmarks for good parenting. Fear of our biological clock will blind us.

Fear of Not Finding the "Right One"
Cliff and Cynthia

Cynthia, age 21, was a single mother. Her baby's father, Cliff, came in and out of her life. Cynthia had a steady job and her mother tended to Cynthia's child when Cynthia was at work. Cynthia described her life as "hard, unexciting, and sometimes boring." It centered on her child and work. The only time Cynthia found herself having "fun" was when her baby's daddy was around. Then they would do activities as a family. However, Cynthia's "fun" was tempered by her resentment that Cliff rarely paid child support and came and went as he pleased without feeling any responsibility toward helping her raise their child.

One day during one of Cliff's rare visits, he asked Cynthia to marry him. Cynthia did not question the motives of this person who had told her that he liked his freedom and was "not the marrying kind." When Cliff proposed, the "dream" flashed through Cynthia's mind: Cliff would be an attentive parent and help her raise their child. Cynthia wisely told Cliff that she would have to think about his proposal. Then Cliff disappeared to "take care of some business." He didn't return for a month.

During that time, Cynthia sought some counseling about what she should do. She reported that she thought, *Cliff is the best I can get. What guy would ever want a coffeehouse barista with one kid? I think Cliff is the only one who will ever want me. The devil I know is better than the devil I don't know.*

If Cynthia decided to marry Cliff, she would lose a chance to find someone who will be a much more supportive partner. She would lose the opportunity to find someone who wanted to be with her and her child. She would spend a lot of time trying to form a family with someone who has already shown her he is not a family man.

Cynthia rationalized, *He has changed, he asked me to marry him!* But Cynthia never did ask, "Why now?" "What business are you cleaning up?" "How are our finances going to be evenly split?" "Are you planning to stay at home with us?" "What are your thoughts about how you want to raise our child?" Cynthia never did address Cliff's propensity to want to "go out and party" with his "homeboys" and the times when he showed up at her home so drunk that she had to put him to bed.

She decided to take a risk. She declined Cliff's marriage proposal and decided to focus on raising her child. She discovered she was much happier. She didn't *settle*! Cynthia realized that if she married Cliff, she would be marrying all the negatives that came with him. Without Cliff, she could raise her child in a stable home, even if it was without a dad.

Three years later, Cynthia left a voicemail on her counselor's phone. She reported that she had found a "fabulous guy" who "loves my child and loves me. I have never been in such a loving relationship. I am calling to let you know how grateful I am that you supported me in not settling for Cliff. Thank you."

One of the reasons we settle for less than kind, stable, and loving romantic relationships is based on our fear that we won't find the "right one." So many of us "settle." We tell ourselves, *No one is perfect*. We are right! No one *is* perfect. But somewhere on the spectrum between perfect and totally unacceptable there is an area that meets our comfort level. It is comprised of "awesome," "fun," "trust," "commitment to our relationship," "disappointing," and "mistakes" (and many more elements). Don't settle for someone whom you can't put in the middle of your criteria for "okayness." If you do, you are *settling*, and that is usually based on fear that you won't find someone better—the "right one."

Fear of Never Having the Fantasy Dream Wedding
Chelsea

At age nine, Chelsea had dreamed of walking down the aisle in a flowing white dress and holding a bouquet of red roses. Each step toward the altar would bring her closer to her Prince Charming, with whom she would live happily ever after. This dream followed Chelsea into adulthood.

Now Chelsea was 23. She had been in a relationship with Jeff for three years. He had "finally" proposed, and Chelsea now found herself on a teeter-totter between creating her dream wedding and coming to terms with all the things she didn't like about Jeff. Chelsea was torn between her long-term dream and her short-term (in comparison) beau.

Chelsea decided that this was the *one* opportunity she would ever have to be the bride in a lavish wedding. After all, who knew what would happen in the future? Maybe her father would die and she wouldn't be able to have him walk her down the aisle. Maybe the economy would crash or her dad would lose his job and wouldn't be able to afford anything as glamorous as Chelsea wanted. Maybe her sister would be pregnant and wouldn't want to be her matron of honor. Chelsea lived in her dream and sorted out all the possible obstacles to making it come true. She didn't focus on what life with Jeff would be like, even though their three years together weren't as wonderful as Chelsea had hoped. She told herself that once they were husband and wife and living together, *everything would sort itself out.*

Chelsea married Jeff. They fought on their honeymoon because Jeff drank too much. They moved into their new apartment. Chelsea arranged the furniture and put their wedding presents away. Jeff watched sports on TV. Chelsea wondered if she had made a mistake.

Having the "dream wedding" will not provide you with a "dream relationship." Projecting out into the future and making up stories about why the "dream wedding" must happen at the first opportunity has led to many unhappy relationships. Think about your future: there you are with your "dream wedding" photo album. You look at it over and over again. Then you look at your partner who is not sitting there with you reminiscing. Like Chelsea, you might realize you are alone in your relationship and in your memories of your "dream wedding."

Fear of Being the Last Single Person in Your Group of Friends

So many young adults rush into a relationship hoping it will turn into a marriage because all their friends are married and are now starting to have children. Think of yourself out to dinner with all your friends. Instead of talking about work, sports, vacations, school, politics, etc., the conversation has now switched to pregnancy, decorating the nursery, baby showers, an infant's sleep patterns, and toilet training. There you are—bored out of your mind. There you are—the last remaining "unattached" person in your group of friends. There you are—without any prospects! There you are—thinking, *What's wrong with me?* There you are, haunted by that old saying, "Always a bridesmaid, never a bride!"

We do *not* need to rush into a relationship because all of our friends are no longer unattached. Find new interests. Make additional friends—notice the sentence is not "Make new friends"; it is *"make additional friends."* Honor yourself for who you are. We can all focus on who we aren't: not married, not in a serious relationship, not raising kids, etc. If we spotlight who we are, and not use our married pals as a measure for that, we will not be driven to make relationship decisions based on "keeping up with the Joneses."

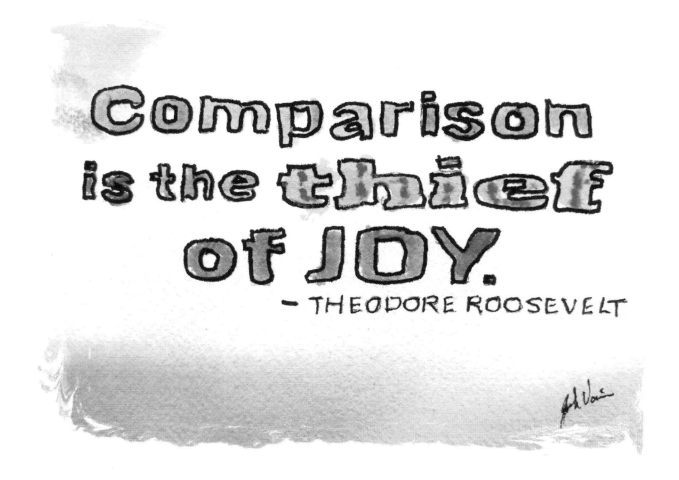

Believing a Relationship Will Complete Me

Each and every one of us tends to enjoy someone who has attributes we don't have. For those of us who are rather quiet, we are often attracted to those who we feel are more interesting and more entertaining than we are. For those of us who are on the talkative side, we sometimes like those who will just listen to us. I guess that old adage "opposites attract" may still be valid.

If we become romantically attracted to someone to "fill our empty spaces," we are not entering into a romance as a whole person. We are entering a relationship as someone who feels they need the other person to make them something they are not or to offset their perceived deficiencies.

Lori and Sandra

Lori, age 24, met Sandra, age 32. For Lori, it was "love at first conversation." Lori watched Sandra at a business party. She studied Sandra as she made her way around the room, greeting people who were there. She was funny, intelligent, engaging, and an easy conversationalist. Sandra was a vice president of the company. Lori was a research physician.

Lori viewed herself as a quiet, boring underachiever who was somewhat of a loner. She felt uncomfortable talking to other people she did not know well. Lori felt an instant attraction to Sandra because not only was she pretty, but she was everything Lori was not.

Sandra came over to Lori and introduced herself. She told Lori she had seen her around but didn't know her position in the company. Lori shyly told her about what she did in her capacity as a research physician. This topic appeared to interest Sandra very much, so she invited Lori to a nearby chair and continued to ask her about how she came to be a doctor, where she went to medical school—the usual meet-and-greet cocktail party conversation.

During their chat, Lori noticed how grateful she was feeling because she didn't have to initiate any topics to discuss. Lori felt comfortable because Sandra had such energy and enthusiasm around Lori's profession. Sandra invited Lori to dinner. Their relationship began. Lori became the listener. Sandra became the extroverted and entertaining talker.

In a conversation with her therapist about her relationship with Sandra, Lori expressed that "Sandra completes me. She's everything I am not. She makes up for my quietness and my tendency to be boring. I just love that about her!"

Over time, Lori's therapist worked with Lori's self-image—just why Lori thought she had deficits and needed to be "completed."

If we enter a relationship because we deem it fills up some lack we perceive ourselves as having, we become dependent on the other person to "make us whole." This usually ends up being very disappointing because only *you* can make *you* whole. You are complete just as you are. You just have to believe it.

Believing a Relationship Will Give Definition to My Life

Wendy and Ralph

Wendy was 35 years old. She claimed that she still didn't know what career she wanted, or if she wanted to get married, or if she wanted to have children. Wendy had zoomed through five different careers: real estate agent, dental assistant, x-ray technician, Zumba instructor at her local gym, and third grade teaching assistant. Wendy viewed some of them as satisfying, some of them as "too hard," and the rest as boring. Wendy feared that she would never find a meaning to her life. She told her mother that she was afraid of being a career nomad.

Wendy's best friend introduced her to her husband's friend Ralph, who worked with him at a prestigious law firm. Ralph specialized in family law, and Wendy loved hearing about all the legal disputes Ralph's clients faced during their divorces.

Over the next year, Wendy and Ralph talked about having a committed relationship. Wendy told her girlfriend that she hoped they would marry because "finally I'll have a real life! I'll be married to a lawyer. I'll belong to Lawyer's Wives! It will be such fun! I'll be Mrs. Ralph Holmes, Esq.'s wife!"

Notice that Wendy is looking to Ralph and his career to define her life because she has not found meaning for it herself. Part of Wendy's love for Ralph is about what he *does*, not who he *is*.

Wendy and Ralph married after three years of dating. Wendy became very active in Lawyer's Wives. She began studying criminal justice at the local junior college so she would be able to discuss Ralph's cases more articulately. A year after they married, Ralph decided he hated law and he wanted to become something totally different—he wasn't sure just what.

Wendy's world crumbled. She imagined losing "everything"! No longer would she be a member of Lawyer's Wives, and why bother studying anything having to do with the law? She considered, *maybe I should just become a mother?*

Find out who *you* are and how *you* can provide definition to your life. If you don't, you can find yourself lost in a sea of possibilities that are provided by someone else. If we let someone else's life/career/interests usurp our privilege to investigate our own passions and define our own lives, we will be disengaging from our authentic selves. This can lead to depression, restlessness, and serial relationships.

External Pressures: Everyone Loves Your Date

Diana and Tres

Diana was a 40-year-old divorced mother of two. Her elderly parents were very concerned about her. They worried that Diana was all alone trying to raise two boys. Her ex-husband, Charlie, did as little as possible to engage with his eight- and ten-year-old sons. Diana's mother's most fervent wish was that Diana would meet someone who would be a good husband and father to her children, someone who would take care of her daughter.

When Diana met Tres, she was very impressed. After a few dates she and Tres settled into a comfortable "getting to know you" friendship. About three months after they met, Diana's mother invited Diana to include Tres at the family Thanksgiving dinner.

From the moment Diana's family set eyes on Tres, they knew that he was the one for her. Tres was tall, handsome, impeccably dressed, and he and Diana "looked like the perfect couple." Tres had a good job and drove the latest-model Mercedes-Benz. That was all Diana's family knew—and that was enough for them!

As time went on, Tres was invited to participate in all the family gatherings for Christmas and New Year's. Diana's mother lobbied for Diana to "fill us in on what's going on with you two. Any announcements that you want to tell us about?" Diana felt pressured. She was unsure that she and Tres were actually compatible. Tres had a history of cheating on his ex-wife and on several of his girlfriends. He had told Diana, "I strayed because each of them just wasn't the right one."

On the other hand, Diana thought that she might be "different than the others"! She and Tres had such fun together, and he was so nice to her sons. Maybe her family was a better judge than she was about who would be right for her. *After all*, Diana told herself, *look what happened when I didn't listen to their warnings and married Charlie.*

After four months of intermittent dating, Charlie had asked Diana to marry him. He told Diana he loved her and that he was "made to be married." Based on her own self-doubts about being able to select men with a good character, Diana accepted. Diana's family was ecstatic. They threw a huge party for the newly engaged couple. Everything was "perfect." And then Diana discovered that Charlie had been living with his sister because his divorce wasn't final; he had an 18-month-old daughter whom he rarely saw; Charlie had been separated from his wife for six months; during his separation, he had five girlfriends.

Diana had ignored her intuitions that there was "something about Charlie that just didn't ring true." She had been blindsided not only by the "love cocktail" and a partner who was influenced by his obsession to find a new partner (limerence), but by her family. Luckily for Diana, she got unengaged, much to her family's disgruntlement.

If we succumb to the influence of our friends and family, we are often pushed into making bad choices for ourselves. *You* need to be the person who decides whom you want as a committed partner, and no one else—unless you let them.

Pregnancy

In the moment, without thought to the ramifications of our behavior, many of us have unprotected sex. We open ourselves to STDs and pregnancy. Others of us are in committed relationships and we find ourselves unexpectedly pregnant. We may have been taking birth control and still find ourselves pregnant.

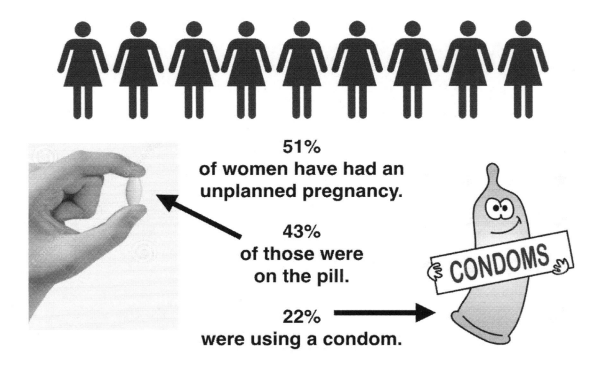

**51%
of women have had an
unplanned pregnancy.**

**43%
of those were
on the pill.**

**22%
were using a condom.**

CONDOMS

With unexpected pregnancies come questions about adoption and abortion. We rush to define our relationship—a one-night stand? Someone I like but would never want to marry? A loving and kind individual who will be a wonderful partner in the long run? We berate ourselves for not taking the morning-after pill, or for not having our partner wear a condom. We obsess about what our partner will say when we deliver the news. What will our families say?

What Do Women (by Race) Facing Unintended Pregnancy Choose?[13]

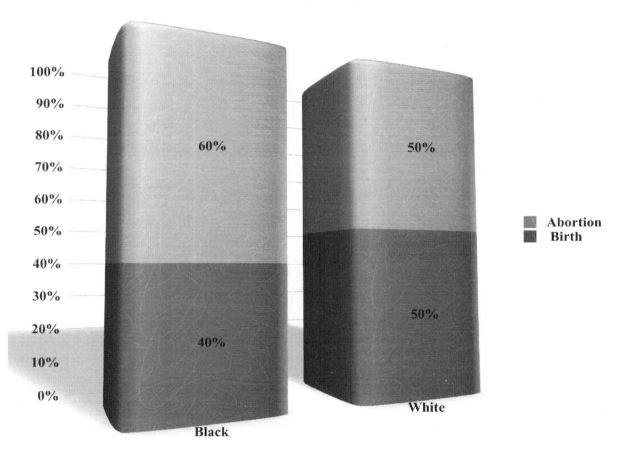

While pregnancy is just one of many reasons that people rush into relationships, it is the one that comes with the most complications. Pregnancy involves more than just one person, and it is ruled by cultural mores, the emotions of peripheral people, and family pressure. Those of us who are not in a committed relationship often pressure the father because "I want my baby to have a dad."

Before the 1960s, "unwed mothers" were often considered to have low morals, hence the push to wed; to eradicate the moral transgression overrode the idea of "love." In current times, "single parenting" is much more accepted. However, unexpected pregnancy remains one main reason to marry.

---

[13] *http://abortioneers.blogspot.com/2010/06/want-to-talk-about-black-women-and.html.*

Percentage of All Births That Were to Unmarried Women, by Age: 2014[14]

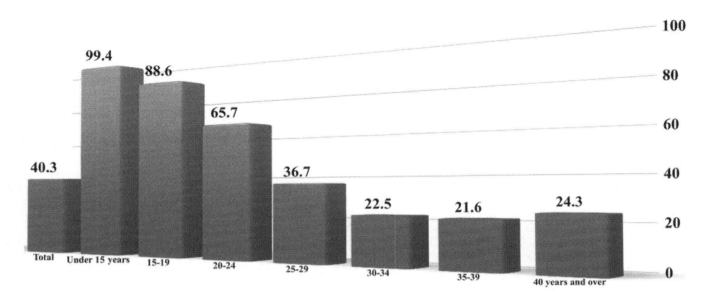

When in that sexual moment, many of us do not consider if an unexpected pregnancy will come with a committed relationship. But when the "news" is shared it creates stress and/or crisis. In the end, some men marry to "do the right thing." Others don't marry, but parent and support their child. Some walk away with the thought, *this is not* my *problem*. Having pregnancy as the main reason for a legal union doesn't usually sustain. Pregnancy cannot provide the foundation of that "happy family" dream when there is not a healthy relationship to underpin it.

---

[14] *U.S. Department of Health and Human Services, Centers for Disease Control and Prevention, National Center for Health Statistics, National Vital Statistics Reports 64, no. 12 (December 23, 2015), https://www.cdc.gov/nchs/data/nvsr/nvsr64/nvsr64_12.pdf.*

Feels Like Home

Terri and Pete

Terri met Pete at a sports bar. Terri was with some girlfriends, and Pete was with his fellow 49er fans watching the game, sharing pitcher after pitcher of beer. Terri watched Pete become drunk. At the end of the game she walked over to him and offered him a ride home. Terri was quite attractive, and Pete's friends considered her offer a "touchdown," so they encouraged him to accept her invitation. Terri dropped Pete at his apartment and then went to her house, where she lived with her parents. There she found her dad with all his tipsy buddies also watching football. Her mother was busy brewing coffee and making sandwiches so her husband's friends wouldn't drive home while under the influence.

Terri and Pete began dating. Pete and some of his pals joined Terri's dad and his friends in the Sunday football watching group. Pete fit in with her family just perfectly. Pete and Terri got engaged. In so many ways Pete felt like "home."

Then Terri took a class about relationships. She learned that just because Pete fit in with her family didn't mean that he was a good match for her. She began to explore her feelings about the fact that every Sunday her dad either hosted or went to other people's homes to watch sports. This practice always led to her dad drinking too much and passing out when his "Sports Club" was over. Terri realized she was very angry about this because her mother spent her Sundays either waiting on her husband's pals or being by herself. Terri realized she did not want a future where weekends were dictated by what was on TV. She discovered that she did not want to live her mother's life. Terri's dad was very upset when she ended her engagement to Pete. "He was the perfect guy to fit into our family," Terri's dad lamented when she told him the news.

There is nothing nicer than to have our love interest fit in with our family of origin. However, if we have rushed into a relationship just because "they fit in so perfectly," it is time to step back and see if the dynamic they fit in with, is the dynamic *you* want to carry forward in your life.

Codependency

Codependency is a very complicated subject. For the purposes of explaining why people rush into unhealthy relationships while under the influence of the "love cocktail" and limerence let's simplify how codependency can take over a relationship.

Many of us love to fix, rescue, give advice, and save others from the consequences of their poor choices. We "fall in love" and then spend the rest of the relationship/marriage telling our partner what they need to change about themselves. All this "control" gives us an ego boost. Think about this: if I can give you advice, it puts me in the "one-up position," and concurrently gives the covert message that you aren't smart enough to solve their issue yourself. Codependency causes inequitable relationships.

Codependents want to be *needed*. The problem is that when we get into a relationship with a needy person, we allow ourselves to get sucked dry. We give and give—advice, helpfulness, money, etc. But we don't give freely. What we codependents expect is gratitude and acknowledgment for our "kindness." When that is not forthcoming—and it usually isn't—we get resentful. We harbor and repress those resentments. We believe that if only the person we care about would change those few items that need fixing, then we would all be happy!

I've never seen this happen. I have seen this type of relationship lead to years of suffering and unhappiness.

Leslie and Paul

Leslie and Paul have been married for two years. They dated six months before that. They were "madly in love" when they married. They had not taken time to notice each other's faults, or to actually get to know each other well. Leslie knew that Paul had one child and had been married to a woman he called "Godzilla." Paul described his ex-wife as a "nag from hell." Leslie didn't think to investigate this more because she was blinded by limerence. She was obsessed with Paul and getting him to "love her."

After three weeks of "blissful marriage," Leslie noticed that Paul did not pick up after himself: he didn't put his dirty dishes in the dishwasher, he left his dirty clothes on the floor, and the mail was spread all over the house. Paul watched TV and played video games in his spare time.

Leslie wanted to "help" Paul. She bought bins so he would have a place to store his mail. She moved the dirty clothes hamper from the bathroom to Paul's closet so he wouldn't have to walk so far when changing his clothes. She tried to negotiate with him to rinse his dishes and put them in the dishwasher. Paul called her a "nag."

Leslie took on the project of lecturing Paul about the benefits of "being neat" and "having a neat home to come to after a long day at work." Paul told Leslie that he liked clutter. He told her that he had never been a "neatnik" and that she was turning into his ex-wife with "all the nagging and tidying up!"

Leslie also discovered that Paul rarely saw his five-year-old daughter. She asked about this and was advised to "mind your own business." In an effort to "mend" relationships and to "get Paul to be a better father," Leslie called Paul's ex-wife, Bernice, and invited her to coffee. Over coffee, Leslie learned that Paul had never paid child support, or remembered his daughter's birthday, or had given her gifts on holidays and special occasions. Leslie became determined to "help" Paul be a good dad.

Over the next few months, Leslie began her campaign to "fix" the relationship between Paul and his daughter and his ex-wife. She did not consider that Paul actually did want to abdicate all responsibility for his child and ex-wife and that he was just "fine" having no contact with them. When he found out about Leslie's meeting with Bernice, Paul was furious. He accused Leslie of being a "meddler," and told her to stay out of his business.

"But, honey," Leslie tearfully responded to his rant, " I'm just trying to help; I want to help you repair relationships so we'll all be happier." Having Paul be tidier and have a relationship with his daughter became Leslie's *project*. Leslie felt unfulfilled because she could not convince Paul that he needed to change, and Paul felt chronically criticized. Leslie felt "empty" and "unhappy." Paul felt "nagged" and "angry."

After their divorce, Leslie quickly found a new *project*, and Paul again found someone who strove to "make me a better person." The cycle goes on and on and usually ends in suffering, dissatisfaction, and emotional exhaustion for both parties.

A New Relationship Diverts Us from Our Problems

When limerence and the "love cocktail" take over we are able to focus on little else. Not only do we lose the ability to make good decisions, but it seems like our life is derailed. We meet a love interest and we abdicate from our responsibilities, our commitments, our hobbies, and our growth as a person! We *want* to think about our "loved" one, who becomes the organizing principle for all our decisions. We unconsciously take a vacation from our problems because it is much more momentarily emotionally rewarding. Let's look at Spenser and Carolyn, who are wonderful examples of how finding and forming a new relationship distracts from a growth process that is usually lifesaving.

Spenser and Carolyn

Spenser is 48 years old. He has been in recovery from substance abuse for five months. During that time, Spenser has had to look at the misery his addictions have brought into the lives of his family members, friends, and business associates. It is painful and agonizing. Spenser would like to avoid this part of recovery and just focus on not drinking and using drugs.

One day he is sitting in a recovery meeting, and a person he has never seen there before sits down next to him. Spenser thinks she is very attractive, and starts a conversation. He learns that her name is Carolyn and that she has 30 days off alcohol, and is struggling with her sobriety. She shares some of her history and how she came to be in recovery. Spenser offers to take her to a meeting he knows about that is really fun and has very interesting speakers.

A few days later they meet again at the AA meeting, and afterward Spenser invites her to coffee. There, he learns that Carolyn is going through a traumatic divorce. Carolyn shares that her children are "acting out," that her family lives far away, and that she feels very alone. Within a month, Spenser and Carolyn are in a relationship. They have bonded through the process of discovering mutual problems.

Spenser switches his focus from sobriety to Carolyn. Carolyn does the same. Their relationship distracts each of them from facing and dealing with the consequences of their respective addictions. The focus on each other diverts them from their problems and becomes a mecca of avoidance. Eventually they return to drinking.

Avoidance of problems through a new relationship does not provide a firm or healthy foundation. But it certainly feels good until those problems come crashing down on us.

Sex/Relationship Addiction

Love and relationship addicts hate being alone. They loathe being dejected. Their life revolves around searching for that special someone—that elusive soulmate. Emotional intimacy with another person is not the goal. The aim is to experience the intense feelings that come with "falling in love." The belief that accompanies this is that falling in love makes them whole. The organizing principle for the relationship/sex addict is the *search* for "the one." The search can affect how they live their lives; doing activities or developing hobbies that provide opportunities for conversation with others is usually a mainstay in the relationship/sex addict's life.

With relationship/sex addicts, limerence and the "love cocktail" provide the "high" that leads the addict to feel on top of the world. That is how folks with this addiction know they have found "the right one"! But the high doesn't last, so the search continues—over and over again.

Given all of the information you have just absorbed, if you are a sex/relationship addict, what about making a contract with yourself? Read the agreement part every day. That way, your brain will begin to store the agreement information so when you are tempted to rush into a romantic relationship, you will have established a braking system for yourself that is etched in your memory.

> **NOTE:** All contracts in this book are available in electronic form to download, modify, and print. See page 212 for more information.

Contract with Yourself for Not Rushing into Relationships

Agreement	Why?	Consequences
I will get to know someone for at least _____ months before getting into a committed relationship.	I want to really know if the person I make a commitment to is someone I can respect, trust, etc.	Unknowingly selecting a mate who doesn't share my values and goals.
I will wait to have sex for _____ (weeks, months), or cohabitation, engagement, marriage.	After having sex, I don't want to be in a relationship with a person I don't know well.	Discovering I don't like the person I am having sex with.
I will review 11 reasons people rush into relationships to see if I fit in any of those categories before considering having sex or committing to a romantic relationship.	To avoid basing my romantic relationships on my neediness, my fears, my tendencies to not face my problems, etc.	Establishing relationships based on *my* character trait(s) that don't lead to happy, stable romantic relationships.
I will review my relationship history to try to discern if they were highly influenced by limerence or the "love cocktail."	If I don't do this work I could fall into cyclical relationships based on a "chemical" and limerent foundation.	Serial disappointing relationships.

CHAPTER 2

What Do I Want in a Romantic Partner?

From the first chapter, we can surmise that when people get into a romantic relationship many of them don't know each other very well. But if you did give yourself the opportunity to get to know someone before deciding to get into a relationship with them, what would you look for?

When considering what one would want in a romantic relationship many of us aren't quite clear about what we *do* want. So often I hear, "I'll know him/her when he/she comes along."

THERAPIST: How will you know?

PATIENT: I'll just know.

THERAPIST: What qualities will you be looking for?

PATIENT: You know, humor, a job.

THERAPIST: Is that all?

Pause… Pause… Pause…

PATIENT: Well, I know what I don't want!

THERAPIST: What is that?

PATIENT: I don't want someone who is uneducated, violent, who lies, and who cheats.

THERAPIST: So are you telling me you want someone who is educated, who is able to handle angry emotions in an appropriate way, who is honest, and who is sexually and emotionally faithful to you?

Pause… Pause… Pause…

PATIENT: I had never thought of it that way.

THERAPIST: Is there anything else that is a requirement when considering a potential relationship?

PATIENT: I don't usually "consider." It just happens. We have fun, we share our likes and dislikes, we have sex, then a relationship starts.

THERAPIST: Has that worked out for you with past relationships?

PATIENT (sadly): No. Sometimes. I don't know. No.

THERAPIST: Do you have any ideas about why this has been your experience?

PATIENT: I get into relationships pretty fast. I don't really know much about them other than they have a good job and are good in bed. Sometimes I meet their parents, but I figure their parents aren't in our relationship—so I don't actually care about if I meet them or not.

THERAPIST: Do you tell your potential relationship what your relationship values are? Do you ask about theirs?

PATIENT: No.

And so it goes. If these answers somewhat reflect your experience with romantic relationships, I suggest that you complete the worksheet on the next few pages.

Let's start with "Traits I Don't Want" because these seem more easily accessed. What we don't want is often an accumulation of negative experiences from past romances or from painful circumstances that have befallen our family and friends.

Worksheet About Traits I Don't Want in a Romantic Relationship

Cheater

Were you ever cheated upon in a previous relationship?

☐ Yes

☐ No

Did you remain in that relationship or in any relationship with someone who had a history of cheating in past marriages or relationships no matter what the reason?

☐ Yes

☐ No

Liar

Were you ever lied to in a previous relationship?

☐ Yes

☐ No

Did you remain in that relationship or in any romantic relationship with someone who did not tell you the truth?

☐ Yes

☐ No

Rager

Were you ever in a romantic relationship in which someone was unable to control rage or anger?

☐ Yes

☐ No

Did you stay in that relationship or in any romantic relationship with someone who exhibited rage and inappropriate anger?

☐ Yes

☐ No

Deadbeat Dad

Were you ever in a romantic relationship in which someone was unable or unwilling to pay child support and did not engage with their child or children on a regular basis?

☐ Yes

☐ No

Did you remain in that relationship or in any romantic relationship in which someone didn't support and engage with their biological offspring no matter what their reason?

☐ Yes

☐ No

Substance Dependence or Behavioral Addiction

Have you ever been in a romantic relationship with someone who has an active addiction to alcohol, marijuana, or other mind-altering substances, or who is addicted to gambling, sex, shopping, or food?

☐ Yes

☐ No

Did you remain in that relationship or in any relationship in which your partner was actively addicted to substances or behaviors?

☐ Yes

☐ No

Substance Use

Have you ever been in a romantic relationship in which their being drunk or high bothers you?

☐ Yes

☐ No

Did you remain in that relationship or in any romantic relationship in which substance use was an issue?

☐ Yes

☐ No

Debt

Have you ever been in a romantic relationship in which your partner was more than a few thousand dollars in debt?

☐ Yes

☐ No

Did you remain in that relationship or in any romantic relationship with someone who had a lot of debt?

☐ Yes

☐ No

What is the amount of debt someone would have to be in for you to consider it "a lot"?

$_____

Did you remain in that relationship or in any romantic relationship in which your partner's debt negatively impacted your ability to do activities as a couple?

☐ Yes

☐ No

Unemployment

Have you ever been in a romantic relationship with someone who didn't have a job?

☐ Yes

☐ No

Did you remain in that relationship or in any romantic relationship with someone who was jobless?

☐ Yes

☐ No

For how long?

Number of months: _____

Lack of Respect

Have you ever been in a romantic relationship in which you didn't admire your partner?

☐ Yes

☐ No

Did you remain in that relationship or in any romantic relationship with someone who you didn't admire?

☐ Yes

☐ No

Lack of Empathy

Have you ever been in a romantic relationship with someone who wouldn't take the time to listen to your life challenges in a supportive and understanding manner?

☐ Yes

☐ No

Did you remain in that relationship or in any romantic relationship with someone who didn't have the ability to understand your feelings and experiences from your perspective?

☐ Yes

☐ No

Verbal Abuse

Have you ever been in a romantic relationship with someone who called you names, blamed you so as to not take their own personal responsibility, put you down, or corrected you as a means of control?

☐ Yes

☐ No

Did you remain in that relationship or in any romantic relationship with someone who verbally abused you?

☐ Yes

☐ No

For how long?

Number of months: _____

Emotional Abuse

Have you ever been in a romantic relationship in which you felt humiliated, intimidated, verbally assaulted, verbally bullied, or made to feel inferior by your partner?

☐ Yes

☐ No

Did you remain in that relationship or in any romantic relationship in which there was a power imbalance in the relationship?

☐ Yes

☐ No

For how long would you stay? _____

Physical Abuse

Have you ever been in a relationship in which your partner intentionally hit, slapped, punched, or caused you physical harm?

☐ Yes

☐ No

Did you remain in that relationship or in any romantic relationship in which your partner caused you physical harm?

For how long would you stay? _____

The topics that have been listed above are usually those that most people *do not want* in a romantic relationship. There are 13 highlighted topics. Check the ones listed below that *you* do not want in a romantic relationship:

☐ Cheater

☐ Liar

☐ Rager

☐ Deadbeat Dad

☐ Substance Dependence or Behavioral Addiction

☐ Substance Use

☐ Debt

☐ Unemployment

☐ Lack of Respect

☐ Lack of Empathy

☐ Verbal Abuse

☐ Emotional Abuse

☐ Physical Abuse

From the list immediately above, how many did you check? _____

You have now defined the attributes you *do not want* in a romantic relationship. Write them down on a separate piece of paper and stick this list in your wallet. Review it often. Feel free to add to this list.

Write down the number of "yes" answers to the questions beginning "Have you ever…": _____
This represents the number of categories that you *do not want* in a romantic relationship, but that you have allowed in. You have ignored your "Don't Want" criteria.

Now total the number of "yes" responses to the second part of each topic that begin "Did you stay" or "Did you remain…"
Write the number here: _____
This represents the number of "Don't Want" categories in which you stayed. You lived with them in a romantic relationship. You did not respect your own "Don't Want" list.

Were any of your "yes" responses present in your family of origin?
Number of "yes" responses: _____

Check the categories of "Don't Wants" that were in your family of origin.
☐ Cheater
☐ Liar
☐ Rager
☐ Deadbeat Dad
☐ Substance Dependence or Behavioral Addiction
☐ Substance Use
☐ Debt
☐ Unemployment
☐ Lack of Respect
☐ Lack of Empathy
☐ Verbal Abuse
☐ Emotional Abuse
☐ Physical Abuse

The "Don't Want" categories that were in your family of origin will feel familiar. These are the ones that can blindside us—we may not recognize them until we are deeply entrenched in a romantic relationship. Upon realization that we are with someone who reminds us of a family member who has been abusive, unsupportive, critical, etc., in our past, we say to ourselves, "Oh my God! I'm in a relationship with my father, mother, aunt, uncle, etc." Use caution. We do not want to repeat in the present the "don't wants" that we hated during our childhood.

Worksheet About Traits I Do Want in a Romantic Relationship

It would be easy to look at the "Don't Want" list and just use that for a template about what we "Do Want" in a romantic relationship. For example, we could think, "I don't want a liar. I want someone who is honest." That would be too easy. We have to come to terms with three things:

- First: *No one is perfect!*
- Second: What are my values and which of them are most important to me?
- Third: We need to define the concept of "settling."

No One Is Perfect!

What does the concept of "perfect" actually mean? To many, it means that the other person doesn't have the behaviors that irritate us and that he/she matches / exceeds / fills our emotional, financial, conversational, spiritual, sexual, etc., needs; shares our values; and enjoys "fun" the same way we do. With the confluence of "doesn't irritate me" and "meets my needs," a "perfect" union can be made! But that is just not true!

Why? Because, if we reread the definition above, it focuses on just one person's irritation triggers and "needs met" criteria. What about the other person in the relationship? Am I "perfect" for them? This type of egocentricity is noninclusive. It doesn't consider that there are *two* people in the relationship. It only considers *you*. No one is perfect or part of an absolutely perfect match. However, some matches are much better than others.

What Are My Values and Which of Them Are Most Important to Me?

Most of us haven't thought about our values much. Often we arbitrarily adopt the values of the family in which we were raised. When these values become functionally obsolete (they don't work for us anymore or we have different values than the ones of our family of origin) we can get confused because there are no guides that lead us through a challenging decision-making process. For example, if we were raised in a family in which infidelity is considered a mortal sin, but now we find ourselves with a physically impaired mate, what do we do? Are values based on the situation, or are they fixed and inflexible?

Please spend some time with the "Value Sort" provided below. Remember that there are many more values than the ones that are listed here. Feel free to add them to your list.

Draw three columns on a piece of paper. The heading for the first column is "Most Important." The heading for the second column reads "Fairly Important." The heading for the third column is "Not Important." Now read through the list below and place each value in one of those columns.

Value Sort

Most Important	Fairly Important	Not Important

List of Values

Acceptance – to be accepted as I am

Accuracy – to be accurate in my opinions and beliefs

Achievement – to have important accomplishments

Abstinence – not imbibing any mind-altering substances

Adaptability – the ability to adjust oneself readily to different conditions

Adventure – to have new and exciting experiences

Attractiveness – to be physically attractive

Authority – to be in charge of and responsible for others

Autonomy – to be self-determined and independent

Balance – to lead a life with equally distributed activities like sleep, work, fun, exercise, etc.

Beauty – to appreciate beauty around me

Caring – to take care of others

Challenge – to take on difficult tasks and problems

Change – to have a life full of change and variety

Comfort – to have a pleasant and comfortable life

Commitment – to make enduring, meaningful commitments

Compassion – to feel and act on concern for others

Contribution – to make a lasting contribution in the world

Cooperation – to work collaboratively with others

Courtesy – to be considerate and polite toward others

Creativity – to have new and original ideas

Curiosity – a strong desire to know or learn something

Dependability – to be reliable and trustworthy

Duty – to carry out my duties and obligations

Ecology – to live in harmony with the environment

Excitement – to have a life full of thrills and stimulation

Faithfulness – to be loyal and true in relationships

Fame – to be known and recognized

Family – to have a happy, loving family

Fitness – to be physically fit and strong

Flexibility – to adjust to new circumstances

Forgiveness – to be forgiving of others

Friendship – to have close, supportive friends

Fun – to play and have fun

Generosity – to give what I have to others

Genuineness – to act in a manner that is true to who I am

God's Will – to seek and obey the will of God

Growth – to keep changing and growing

Health – to be physically well and healthy

Helpfulness – to be supportive of others

Honesty – to be honest and truthful

Hope – to maintain a positive and optimistic outlook

Humility – to be modest and unassuming

Humor – to see the humorous side of myself and the world

Independence – to be free from dependence on others

Industry – to work hard and well at my life tasks

Inner Peace – to experience personal peace

Intimacy – to have affectionate, close relationships

Justice – to promote fair and equal treatment for all

Knowledge – to learn and contribute valuable knowledge

Leisure – to take time to relax and enjoy

Loved – to be loved by those close to me

Loving – to give love to others

Mastery – to be competent in my everyday activities

Mindfulness – to live conscious and mindful of the present moment

Moderation – to avoid excesses

Monogamy – to have one close, loving relationship

Nonconformity – to question and challenge authority and norms

Nurturance – to take care of and nurture others

Openness – to be open to new experiences, ideas, and options

Order – to have a life that is well-ordered and organized

Passion – to have deep feelings about ideas, activities, or people

Pleasure – to feel good

Popularity – to be well-liked by many people

Power – to have control over others

Purpose – to have meaning and direction in my life

Rationality – to be guided by reason and logic

Realism – to see and act realistically and practically

Recreational Use of Drugs – to use drugs appropriately in social situations

Respect – to be treated with respect and to treat others the same way

Responsibility – to make and carry out responsible decisions

Risk – to take risks and chances

Romance – to have intense, exciting love in my life

Safety – to be safe and secure

Self-acceptance – to accept myself as I am

Self-control – to be disciplined in my own actions

Self-esteem – to feel good about myself

Self-knowledge – to have a deep and honest understanding of myself
Service – to be of service to others
Sexuality – to have an active and satisfying sex life
Simplicity – to live life simply, with minimal needs
Solitude – to have time and space where I can be apart from others
Spirituality – to grow and mature spiritually
Stability – to have a life that stays fairly consistent
Tolerance – to accept and respect those who differ from me
Tradition – to follow respected patterns of the past
Virtue – to live a morally pure and excellent life
Wealth – to have plenty of money
World Peace – to work to promote peace in the world

Study the values you have placed in the left column of your paper. These are the uncompromisable values and the most important ones that the object of your romantic relationship must have in common with you. Couples with different "most important" values often don't see eye to eye in the area of romance and in the making of life or daily decisions. This can easily lead to arguments or worse.

Values Worksheet

Now, with your list of values, do this worksheet for each of the values in the column titled "Most Important" values:

Value: _____

Have you ever been in a romantic relationship with someone who did not share this value?
☐ Yes
☐ No
Did you stay in this romantic relationship?
☐ Yes
☐ No
Were you happy in this relationship after six months?
☐ Yes
☐ No
Were you happy in this relationship after a year?
☐ Yes
☐ No
After how many years (if ever) did this relationship become unhappy? _____
Was the value you wrote above violated?
☐ Yes
☐ No

Values Worksheet Results

Score the "Uncompromisable Values" you ignored.

Total number of values I have ignored: _____

1–2: You are able to set some boundaries regarding staying true to your values. (Unless you have very few values—then look at the last scoring interpretation.)

3–5: You give mixed messages to your relationships about your values. Your partner won't have a clear understanding about which of your values to respect because you don't honor your values as concepts you live by.

6 or more: You violate many of your "Uncompromisable Values." Your partner will have no clear guidelines from which to interact with you. You will allow other people's values to lead your romantic decision-making, and your relationship will probably not be built on a firm foundation.

After completing your Value Sort, did you find that when you are in a romantic relationship you tend to violate your values?

Below, make a list of the values you have ignored.

Add more lines if you have violated more of your values than the list accommodates. Notice how many times you have violated your values. *If we disrespect our "uncompromisable values" why should other people respect them?* When we violate our own values we cannot be serene in a relationship. Usually, we spend a lot of time trying to get our partner to respect our values. This is a waste of time!

Alisa

Alisa is a 39-year-old female. She is college educated and has a job that allows her to aspire to higher positions with increased salaries. Alisa has been in a number of serial romantic relationships—one man after the other, looking for that elusive "soulmate."

In a therapy session, Alisa recalled her three most important romantic relationships:

1. Henry was a mechanic who smoked marijuana daily. He told Alisa that he smoked pot due to back pain. Alisa hated the smell of weed and she felt like Henry was never present in the relationship. Henry broke up with Alisa because she "nagged about my pot habit." In other words, Henry chose marijuana over Alisa—or so she said she felt. They were together three months. Alisa discovered she had broken her value of *moderation*.

2. Charlie was a trainer at Alisa's gym. She loved the looks of his body and the fact that he was physically fit. Charlie criticized Alisa's figure and told her she needed to work out more. He would only eat organic food, did not drink alcohol or use drugs. Charlie was a sports fanatic. When he was not at the gym, Charlie was watching or playing sports. Alisa had discovered she had broken her value of *moderation* and her value of *being accepted for who she was*.

3. Greg was a high-powered business executive. He rarely had time for Alisa because he was "swamped" with work. When they were together it was mostly to have sex and order dinner in. Greg never spent the night with Alisa because he had to get enough sleep to be able to focus on work. Alisa discovered that once again she had ignored her value of *moderation*. She also found that she had violated other values; she wasn't having fun with Charlie, the only intimacy was sexual and Alisa didn't feel loved.

In her search for romance, Alisa repeatedly violated her own values. She recurrently paired with people who perhaps were emotionally unavailable because they were "married" to their drugs, work, or sports activities. Alisa did what I like to call "meet, greet, and commit." She did not screen whom she let into her life and thus she experienced one after another disappointing RRs.

Alisa's Values Contract

Agreement	Why?	Consequences for Breaking My Agreement
Before entering into a romantic relationship (RR) I will do the Value Sort with my prospect.	Because I don't want to repetitively violate my values.	Having an unhappy RR. Arguing about what's "right" and "wrong."
I will date for a year before making a romantic relationship commitment with my prospect.	This will give me time to experience his/her values and to learn how this person treats their RR.	Setting myself up for violating my values and being treated with disrespect.
If my prospect and I don't have five or more values that match my "uncompromisable" values, I will end the relationship or define it as a friendship with no romantic potential.	I want to free myself from trying to have RR with people who are not a match for me.	Having repetitively unhappy relationships and perhaps missing out on someone who is more of a match for me.
I will not have sex with a romantic prospect until we take the Value Sort and discuss it.	Because I do not want to make having sex the main activity in a RR.	Just having sex is *not* having a RR. I will set myself up for being used.

"Settling"

We need to define the concept of "settling." Just what does the term refer to?

Settling is being tired of the search for the "right" guy/girl and getting into a RR by convincing ourselves that no one better will come along. It is the process by which we allow our intuition to be overridden by our worry about the future. When we settle, we abdicate our most important values. We shut off something inside ourselves for another person. Settling does *not* lead to happy romantic relationships, because settling is usually accompanied by a struggle for our own authenticity.

When we settle we don't ask ourselves, *What feels wrong in this RR?* or *Why am I not feeling understood and supported?* With settling, we stay in a relationship and tell ourselves that we are happy, but we might be even happier if our partner would just change some of those behaviors (remember, behaviors are based on values) that rub us the wrong way. We shut down the cautionary thoughts, needs, and feelings inside us for this romantic relationship.

Have you ever told yourself something over and over to the point that you now believe it? Or have any of your family members repetitively told you something about yourself, and you have heard it so often that now you believe it? If you tell yourself over and over that you will have to settle into a RR in which someone else's needs are more important than your own, then suffering becomes the norm.

Many of us who have settled don't call it suffering. We call it "understanding," "acceptance," or "giving help" by providing our RR with something they missed in childhood. We often try to make up for the sad experiences of the person we tell ourselves we love.

Go back to your Value Sheet. Look at column three—those values that are not important to you. Look at column two—those values that are less necessary for your partner to hold. Look at your partner's worksheet. How many of your "not important" values or "less important" values are in his/her first column of "uncompromisable" values? Are you two a match?

Make a list of your uncompromisable values. Put it in your wallet, on your bathroom mirror, in your car. Study it. Use it as a measure from which you will discern the qualities of the next potential romantic relationship you meet. Don't be afraid to walk away.

Now that we have made a list of what we *don't want* and a list of what we *do want* (our most important values), let's take those lists and make the final list with which we will screen our future potential romantic relationships.

Deal Breakers

Just what are romantic relationship deal breakers?

So many of my patients have no idea what their RR "deal breakers" are! Let's define this term. A deal breaker is any factor that is significant enough to terminate a relationship. Look at your value list. A deal breaker is any value (in the "Most Important" column) that is not held in common with a potential romantic relationship. A deal breaker is any behavior that suggests that values are not held in common. This is important because potential relationships can say they hold your same values, but their behavior indicates differently.

Our list of "Don't Wants" are also our deal breakers.

When a potential romantic relationship knowingly or unknowingly violates our deal breakers, *it is time to leave that (potential) romantic relationship.*

Andy and Tim

Andy was looking for a partner. As a gay male he wanted a mate who was openly gay and who shared his passion for living in the Castro District in San Francisco. Andy had a history of being cheated on in other relationships, and these experiences had left him heartbroken. He also desired to be with someone who could afford and enjoyed traveling, and someone who loved to cook.

Andy came for therapy because he had a propensity to select "wild" partners: those who loved to party and occasionally drink too much. He was confused about what he wanted and what he thought he could get. He also recognized that he had a tendency to cling to partners who "made me anxious, sad, and mad."

After doing the Worksheets and Value Sort provided above, Andy discovered that in looking for a potential relationship he had not been in touch with his own values. Instead, he had been enjoying all the fun activities that usually accompany dating. He didn't look any deeper than that, so when he and his "fun dates" entered into a relationship, it quickly fell apart.

He decided that in looking for his next relationship he would first watch for any behaviors that violated his values. Then, Andy planned that after a period of dating, he would require his potential RRs to do the Value Sort with him.

Andy met Tim. Andy was in the limerence and "love cocktail" stage when he was invited over to Tim's house so they could walk together to a restaurant for dinner. Tim opened the door and cautioned Andy to "be careful of the stuff—it's my family's. It means a lot to me."

Andy squeezed himself through the entry hall and into a living room that was piled to the ceiling with boxes, clothes, furniture, stuffed animals, etc. Besides that, Tim's house "reeked"! Tim was a hoarder! This first presentation violated Andy's values of order and cleanliness (Andy had added this last one to the Value Sort because it was an important value to him and was not on the Value Sort list.)

He looked around Tim's house with his mouth agape. He knew he could never live this way. However, all those "love chemicals" and his obsession with Tim as a person told him that "once Tim was away from his house and living somewhere else, he would be neat." They whispered in his ear that "Tim needs me to help him get through this attachment to 'stuff' so we can be together."

Andy had done enough therapy to know that listening to the "love cocktail" and to limerence would not get him what he wanted—a healthy, committed, orderly life with a partner whom he loved and who loved him.

He knew that the way Tim lived was a deal breaker. He kindly turned to Tim and said, "Tim, I like you so much as a person. I hope we can continue to be friends. I have to bow out of any thoughts of us having a romantic, committed relationship though. I could never live like this. Neatness and cleanliness is just one of my requirements of a relationship. I think we are not a match."

Andy's emotions and his words did not match, however. He had to force himself to leave Tim's home. He felt awful afterward. He couldn't eat. He went home and went to sleep feeling very lonely and forlorn.

Now that you have the methods with which to discern what you do want in a relationship, what you don't want, and what your deal breakers are, summarize all your work by completing the following list.

Don't Wants	Values	Deal Breakers

Let's move to examining what unhealthy relationships look like. Many of us have stayed in so many unhealthy partnerships for so long they have begun to look healthy!

CHAPTER 3

Unhealthy Relationships

Many of us know when we are in an unhappy romantic relationship and many of us try to rationalize our feelings of regret and sadness about how it turned out. We often stay in these unhealthy romantic relationships because we want to believe with all our hearts that he/she will change if we just keep reminding them of things they do that cause us unhappiness. Or, we say to ourselves, *Maybe I'm not being very understanding* or, *It won't be this way forever. This person really needs me!*

Sometimes we have had so many unhealthy serial RRs that the unhappy past becomes the criterion for what is used as a measure of "okayness" with a potential romantic relationship (PRR). For example if your past RR hit you and your current one doesn't, that can be a large factor in your decision-making process about future RRs. The problem with this is that we have compiled the qualities of past partners that are *not* "OK," and now we are using those negative characteristics as our decision-making criteria in PRRs. Our measure is based on what we do *not* want instead of what we *do* want. This is rather like going into a car dealership and having the following conversation with the salesperson:

BUYER (looking for a new car): I hate blue cars. The last blue car I had broke down all the time. Don't show me blue cars.
SALESPERSON: What color would you like?
BUYER: I don't know, just not anything blue!
SALESPERSON: Is there anything else you want on this car?
BUYER: Oh yeah! I don't want bench seats. I hate bench seats.
SALESPERSON: Anything else?
BUYER: Just show me some cars; I'll know it when I see it. (Notice this sentence is *not* "I'll know it when I drive it!")

Notice how superficial this is. There is no consideration of what this buyer actually does want. It is all based on negative past experiences with cars. No research has been done about the positive or negatives of the cars being shown. Our information is based on the salesperson… just like our potential new relationship who is interested in us. Only the good parts are shared—it is a sales pitch that is often so good we ignore any red flags.

And, by the way, *we* do the same thing. When we are interested in a PRR, we show our best side—we become the salesperson in hopes that our flaws won't makes us a "rule out" for the person who is holding our interest. We hide out until some type of relationship foundation (usually on sand—often on sex) is built. At some point though, we can't help showing our real selves because we are not able to mask the qualities we have that might be a deal breaker for someone else, forever.

Let's summarize: so far we know about limerence and the "love cocktail." We know that it is probably not wise to rush into a romantic relationship, because we have seen the statistics. We now realize how many times we have stayed in unhappy relationships. We have identified our values. We did the worksheets about what we *do* and what we *don't* want in our romantic relationship(s).

With this information at hand, let's now explore some of the components of unhappy romantic relationships and some of the reasons you stay in your suffering. Yes, that is the word—*suffering*. Isn't that the outcome of unhappy RRs?

What Makes an Unhappy Romantic Relationship?

1. Giving a "pass" to behaviors that aren't OK and violating your own values
2. Substance abuse/dependence
3. Mental health issues
4. Cheating/infidelity
5. Narcissism
6. Hiding your authentic self
7. Making a commitment against one's better judgment
8. The inability to problem-solve
9. Codependency

There may be more items you want to add to this list. If you do add anything, make sure you define it as in the examples below.

Giving a "Pass" to Behaviors That Aren't OK and Violating Your Own Values

When we give a "pass" to behaviors that violate our values, we have trained the person we are with how to treat us. When we give a pass to behaviors that are *not* OK, they become part of our relationship. Why do we give not OK behaviors a pass? Because we want to avoid conflict; we want to have a nice evening; we don't have the energy—and a multitude of other excuses for disrespecting our own values.

To illustrate this, let's use the example of allowing someone to call you a name like "bitch" or "bastard," and having no consequences for these types of insults. If we have an uncompromisable value of "respect," allowing someone to call us names violates that value over and over again. Oh! You are thinking that you get angry when this happens? Then what? Eventually it blows over? Anger is not a consequence, and it doesn't change anything. Having value insults blow over doesn't change anything either.

To continue on with the name calling value insult example, when name calling has become the usual dialogue in a relationship because *you* didn't put a stop to it, name calling becomes OK even though it is not. See how confusing it is? We teach our romantic partners to be confused because we are so unclear and don't respect our own values.

Gary and Lizzie

GARY: Hey, I don't understand why you hate my parents so much. Yeah, they're old, and they could have been nicer to you, but they *are* my parents.

LIZZIE: You didn't stand up for me when we told them we were living together, and they said that you could "do better!" I'm just not going over to their house to visit *ever*!

(Notice value violation #1—Lizzie has a value of being in a relationship with someone who respects her and who will stand up for her. She values compassion and courtesy.)

GARY: Well you don't have to be such a bitch about it!

(Value violation #2—Lizzie abhors name calling; it violates her values of intimacy and respect.)

Lizzie goes out of the room where the argument took place and slams the door without another word. Gary hears the car start and go down the street.

There they are—value violations! Disrespect, lack of compassion, lack of courtesy, and behaviors that break intimacy! The consequence? Anger! Did it solve anything? Probably not.

What would happen if Gary and Lizzie had this alternate dialogue?

GARY: Hey, I don't understand why you hate my parents so much. Yeah, they're old, and they could have been nicer to you, but they *are* my parents.

LIZZIE: You didn't stand up for me when we told them we were living together and they said that you could "do better!" I'm just not going over to their house to visit *ever*!

GARY: Well you don't have to be such a bitch about it!

LIZZIE: I will not be called such demeaning names, ever again. I will not be treated discourteously. I will think what to do about this, but name calling and disrespect in this relationship stops right now. I'm going over to Betty's. I'll see you when you get home from visiting your parents.

Then Lizzie *leaves*! Now is not the time to have a further conversation.

The next day:

LIZZIE: I have been thinking about how I want to be treated by you. I think I never really shared with you that calling me demeaning names and treating me with disrespect and having no compassion violates important values of mine. These inconsiderations have to be extinguished in our relationship. Can you do that?

GARY: I don't know. Whatever. You just make me so mad!

LIZZIE (not taking Gary's bait): Please think about this and let me know, because calling me demeaning names and not standing up for me when someone treats me discourteously only leads to suffering for me, and I don't want that emotional pain. Please let me know how you plan to change this—if indeed you do plan to change it—in the next two days. I will not be asking you about this again. If in two days you haven't opened up a discussion about your thoughts, I am going to believe that no change is forthcoming.

Notice that Lizzie did not hand the power over to Gary (the offender) by asking when he would reply to her request.

Remember, what has no consequence goes into what I like to call the "OK Corral." What hangs out in the "OK Corral" are those behaviors that are *not* OK that we have reinforced because there are no boundaries in place to stop them. Lizzie's job is to put limits in place and to relate what will happen with the next bout of name calling, discourtesy, and lack of compassion.

Delivering a contract could be helpful if talking about this topic is too "high voltage" for this couple.

But examine the last part of this sentence "talking about this topic (a problem) is too high voltage…" If collaboration in problem-solving is a value of Lizzie's, she has violated her own values by getting into and staying in a relationship with someone who is not collaborative and who uses his emotions (name calling, blaming, and shaming to deflect anger) to deal with people who won't do his bidding or who don't agree with him. If this is where you find yourself—having given a pass to behaviors that are *not* OK—*you* will have to be the one to correct the interactions that violate your values. If you are *not* with a person who can discuss problems between you, a contract may help… or it may not! Why wouldn't a contract help? If there are other components (like the ones listed below) in your unhappy RR, one may have to leave the relationship because it is so unhealthy.

Personal values serve five purposes in romantic relationships:
- Values serve as standards for behavior.
- Values provide guidelines for decision-making and conflict resolution.
- Values affect thoughts and actions.
- Values influence motivation and perceptions in romantic relationships.
- Values influence attitudes and behaviors.

What Is Not OK in an Argument?

Here is a list of possible options. Which ones have you given a pass to when you are in a disagreement with your RR? Have you violated a value and allowed someone else to violate one of your values?

Add your own at the end.

Yelling:
- ☐ OK?
- ☐ Not OK?
- ☐ Given it a pass?
- ☐ Violated a value of mine?

Using Disrespectful Language:
- ☐ OK?
- ☐ Not OK?
- ☐ Given it a pass?
- ☐ Violated a value of mine?

Pushing/Hitting:
- ☐ OK?
- ☐ Not OK?
- ☐ Given it a pass?
- ☐ Violated a value of mine

Name Calling:
- ☐ OK?
- ☐ Not OK?
- ☐ Given it a pass?
- ☐ Violated a value of mine?

Throwing Things:
- ☐ OK?
- ☐ Not OK?
- ☐ Given it a pass?
- ☐ Violated a value of mine?

Add Your Own

Behavior_____:
- ☐ OK?
- ☐ Not OK?
- ☐ Given it a pass?
- ☐ Violated a value of mine?

Damaging Property:
- ☐ OK?
- ☐ Not OK?
- ☐ Given it a pass?
- ☐ Violated a value of mine?

Threats of Physical Harm:
- ☐ OK?
- ☐ Not OK?
- ☐ Given it a pass?
- ☐ Violated a value of mine?

Threats of Divorce:
- ☐ OK?
- ☐ Not OK?
- ☐ Given it a pass?
- ☐ Violated a value of mine?

Slamming Doors:
- ☐ OK?
- ☐ Not OK?
- ☐ Given it a pass?
- ☐ Violated a value of mine?

Harming Pets:
- ☐ OK?
- ☐ Not OK?
- ☐ Given it a pass?
- ☐ Violated a value of mine?

Behavior_____:
- ☐ OK?
- ☐ Not OK?
- ☐ Given it a pass?
- ☐ Violated a value of mine?

Add up the Not OK checks: _____

Add up the Given It a Pass checks: _____

Add up the Value Violation checks: _____

Total of all three: _____

The total of these checks is the number of times that you have violated your own boundaries or have allowed someone else to violate them.

Value Violation Contract Example

Agreement	My Responsibilities	Consequences for Breaking Agreements
It is unacceptable to me to be called demeaning names during my relationship with you.	To extinguish my own participation in name calling in this relationship.	Suffering because you allowed your values/boundaries to be violated.
With every episode of name calling, I have made arrangements to spend the night with _____.	To find a friend with whom you can stay on short notice or to rent a hotel rom.	Staying in a volatile situation in which you have been demeaned. Nothing will be solved.
If there are continual episodes of name calling—five or more—I will rent a room/house/apartment/move to a relative's residence and move out.	To make arrangements to vacate residing with someone who violates known boundaries.	To continue giving a "pass" to disrespect and staying in a relationship that knowingly demeans you. This leads to more suffering.
Before I consider moving back, agreements must be in place between us regarding the cessation of disrespectful remarks.	To remain firm about creating agreements that will support your value.	More of the same disrespectful treatment. Without a solution, nothing changes.

Substance Abuse/Dependence

Substance abuse and behavioral addictions inevitably lead to unhappy romantic relationships. Why?

There are millions of people in relationships with people whose primary relationship is actually not with a human; it is with a substance or an addictive behavior! Many of these folks spend years trying to convince the addict in their life to stop using drugs and/or alcohol (DOA) or to stop gambling, workaholism, etc. When DOA and behavioral addiction come between two humans in a relationship, chaos takes over the partnership and the family. We try to monitor the addict's use/behavior. We give advice, plead with them to get treatment, despair when they come home or pick us up for a date drunk or high or extremely late because they got "stuck at work."

Values: Before becoming involved with a potential RR, be clear on *your* values. If you are a substance abuser and like the idea of being with a using person, chances are your relationship will be based around using. This will *never* provide you with a foundation for a healthy relationship.

If you are OK with social use of alcohol/marijuana, define what "social" use means to you. You and your PRR need to be on the same page with this. If drinking a small glass of wine with dinner twice per week is what you think of as "social" imbibing and if your PRR thinks consuming a bottle of wine with dinner is "social" drinking, there is a rather large divergence in perception. Will this ever work out? From my experience, probably not.

If you don't use drugs and your PRR has a long history of drug use but has "stopped," we need to ask more questions. What was your drug of choice? How long have you been clean and sober (abstinent from *all* mind-altering substances, including alcohol)? How do you stay abstinent? If you receive defensive responses, investigate exactly what that is about. Most of the addicts in recovery that I have had the privilege to cross paths with in the last two decades are happy to discuss their recovery and how they have maintained it.

If you never had the DOA discussion with the person in the relationship in which you now find yourself, perhaps it is time to address this issue. Consider the two examples below. In the first one, Brad and Trish have just started to date… they are a potential romantic relationship. In the second example, Suzanne and Hank have been married for five years and Hank has watched Suzanne slowly become more and more involved with marijuana.

Brad and Trish

BRAD: I want to tell you something.
TRISH: What?
BRAD: I used to do drugs.
TRISH: Really?
BRAD: Yea, but I've stopped for six months.
TRISH: How did you do that? Wow, that must have been hard!
BRAD: Not too hard.
TRISH: What did you do to quit?
BRAD: I just stopped. I got a DUI, so I had to go to traffic school.
TRISH: So you haven't used anything for six months?
BRAD: Well, basically, yes. Sometimes I have a drink, but I have it under control.

It is now time for Trish to study addiction or to seek counseling with a therapist who is familiar with addiction and recovery. In this scenario, Brad is *not* in recovery as he is still drinking. What are Trish's values about this? What will it look like to be in a RR with a person with a long substance-abuse history who is not in recovery? What will it look like to be in a relationship with a person who *is* in recovery from drugs/alcohol? Trish has no understanding about addiction. She needs to get one, because otherwise she is signing up for an unhealthy relationship that will be full of unpleasant surprises.

It might be tempting to give someone like Brad a pass because we are ignorant about substance addiction. Make a contract with yourself about what you will do when discovering your PRR has a behavior or condition you know nothing about.

Suzanne and Hank

HANK: Honey, I have noticed that you are smoking a lot of pot lately. This really worries me. What's going on?

SUZANNE: Nothing. I have pain and I have trouble sleeping, so being high helps me.

HANK: It feels like you are retreating from me, and our relationship, and becoming more dedicated to smoking weed.

SUZANNE: Well, you can feel however you want to feel. Just leave me alone. I have a medical marijuana card and that's all I need to know.

HANK: I have come to hate pot smoking, the smell of it that is all over the house, and I really hate what it is doing to you!

SUZANNE (turning to Hank in an aggressive manner): Yeah? Well put your big-boy pants on and get through it 'cuz it's the only thing that helps me, but *you* don't really care about me; all you care about is my pot smoking!

Suzanne walks away so she will not have to participate in this uncomfortable confrontation.

In this conversation there is no problem-solving, and Suzanne really doesn't have to make any changes because Hank went out into the garage to work on a project. If Hank is like many of us who are in a relationship with an addict, he will get on a soapbox about why pot is bad for Suzanne, why she should find alternative ways to deal with her insomnia and pain, how she should do it, etc. Hank might plead with Suzanne to get treatment for cannabis dependence. He might end up ignoring the problem and try to live with it. Without a consequence, there is absolutely no reason for Suzanne to change. Hank's lectures and perhaps anger are no consequence, because Suzanne will shine them on and continue to smoke weed. She might even add Hank to her reasons for using pot.

Areas to be wary about in the area of substance abuse and behavioral addictions are:

1. Gambling
2. Excessive shopping
3. Video gaming
4. Porn on the internet
5. Food addiction
6. Fanaticism about any topic that does not interest you (such as sports, golf, etc.)
7. Workaholism
8. Sex and love addiction
9. Phobias that limit your PRR or RR from participating in things you like to do

10. Codependency: you like your PRR/RR because he/she needs you and you think you can fix him/her. Remember, the only one you can fix is *you*!

Values: Chronic substance abuse and behavior addiction in a relationship will violate intimacy, balance, moderation, openness, responsibility, and respect values (to name a few). Addictions are an issue that will *never* be managed by giving lectures, begging someone to get treatment, crying, avoiding, etc. Addictions require professional help. They require *behavioral* consequences from the person who finds himself/herself in a relationship with an addict.

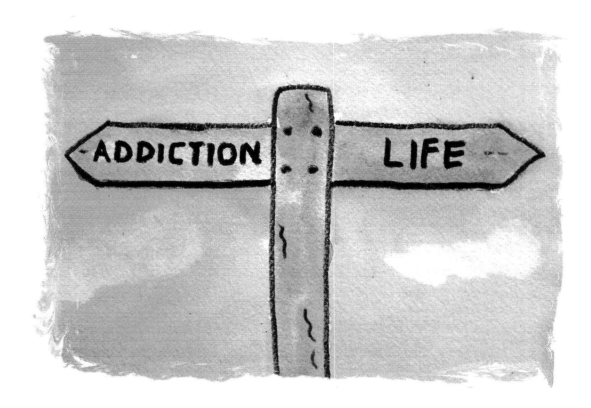

Substance and Behavioral Addiction Violations Contract

Agreement	My Responsibilities	Consequences for Breaking Agreements
When learning my potential RR has a condition/behavior I know nothing about, I will get counseling to learn about the pros and cons of being with someone who has that condition.	Find a specialist in the area of your concern. Go and learn about your potential RR's condition.	You will walk into a relationship without knowing what behaviors are predictable with the condition your potential RR has.
I will read about my PRR's or RR's condition/behavior.	Go to the library/book store/internet and read about your PRR's or RR's condition.	Remaining in ignorance.
Do a Value Sort to determine if any part of my PRR's or RR's behavior/condition conflicts with my values.	To compare (not ignore) the outcome of my Value Sort to my PRR's or RR's behavior caused by his/her condition.	Setting myself up to deal with violations of my values that will lead to my suffering and an unhealthy relationship. Knowingly violating my own values.
If what I learn about the behaviors/risks connected with my potential PRR's or RR's condition conflicts with my values, I will walk away from the potential RR and get counseling for the RR.	To *not* believe that you can put up with behaviors that will violate your values.	Emotional wounds, suffering, frustration, hopelessness, and robbing yourself of an opportunity to find and be in a healthy relationship.

Mental Health Issues

Living with a person who has mental health issues can be very challenging—if that person allows the mental health challenge to run their life. There is a big difference between being with a person with unmediated bipolar disorder and being with someone who has a practiced protocol with which to disallow the condition from running their life. Sure, some mental health challenges are more difficult than others. Interview your potential RR to see how he or she is structuring the care of their mental health condition. Watch for behaviors that suggest that the mental health condition will be an issue for you if you enter into a relationship with them.

If your RR develops a mental health challenge after your romantic relationship has been solidified, work with your partner about how to manage it.

People with mental health challenges have a lot on their plate. Even if substance abuse brought on the condition, no one is ever to be blamed because they have a mental health issue. What must be determined when considering having a romantic relationship with someone who has a mental health challenge is if *you* can live with it long term, and if your PRR is dedicated to not allowing their challenge to run their life.

Bob and Sally

BOB: I want you to know that I was diagnosed with depression last year.
SALLY: Really? What's it like to feel depressed? I have experienced sadness, but I don't think I've ever felt depressed.
BOB: It's like wanting to stay in bed all day with the curtains drawn and being unable to get myself up. It's like being uninterested in anything. I don't eat very much when I'm depressed.
SALLY: What do you do about it?
BOB: Nothing. I just wait for it to pass.
SALLY: How long does that take?
BOB: It depends.
SALLY: On what?
BOB: I don't know.

Clearly, Bob is not taking care of his depression—it is ruling his life. He also has no plan about what to do when he is feeling depressed, and Sally hasn't known him long enough to gauge the real effects of Bob's depression. She would be mistaken to take Bob's explanation of his depression at face value because Bob seems to be making light of it.

Different dialogue:
BOB: I want you to know that I was diagnosed with depression last year.

SALLY: Really? What's it like to feel depressed? I have experienced sadness, but I don't think I've ever felt depressed.

BOB: It's like wanting to stay in bed all day with the curtains drawn. When I'm depressed I don't want to move or do anything. I don't really want to eat and I'm not interested in very much.

SALLY: What do you do about it?

BOB: I have a protocol for what I do when depression wants to take over my life. I make myself exercise every day for 30 to 60 minutes. I spend 20 minutes a day petting Sparky [his dog] because doing that soothes me. I make sure I take my antidepressant as prescribed, and I email my psychiatrist so she knows what is going on with me. I only eat healthy food. I don't consume sugar or caffeine. I allow myself a 30-minute nap on weekends, and I make myself call some people in my depression support group.

SALLY: Wow! It sounds like you are kicking depression in the ass!

BOB: Not always, but I refuse to let it take over my life.

Mental health challenges can bring chaos into a relationship and into a family. They can also be managed. Check your list of uncompromisable values so you can plan how to protect yourself from violations. Make a plan for yourself about how to protect your values. For example, if order (to have a life that is well organized) is an "uncompromisable" value of yours, and your romantic relationship has a diagnosis of bipolar 1 disorder, the manic/depressive moods that accompany this diagnosis can be extremely disruptive. What to do about that so that you still respect your value? (Hint: there is a new therapy dealing with emotion regulation called emotional efficacy therapy—work with your RR to *find it and do it*!)[15]

Mental Health Problems

---

[15] McKay, Matthew, PhD, and Aprilia West, PsyD, *Emotion Efficacy Therapy: A Brief, Exposure-Based Treatment for Emotion Regulation Integrating ACT and DBT* (Context Press, 2016).

Mental Health Challenge
Contract for PRRs

Agreements	My Responsibilities	Consequences for Breaking Agreements
One of the questions I will ask a PRR is if they have a history of mental health (MH) challenges. I will also ask if anyone in his/her family has a MH diagnosis. (Mental health issues can be genetic.)	To ask the question.	Living with a large unknown in your relationship.
I will ask my PRR how they take care of their mental health challenge.	To listen carefully for a MH protocol that my PRR follows in order to diminish the power of the mental health in his/her life.	Finding yourself in a relationship in which a mental health challenge "drives the bus." Not knowing if your PRR's mental health challenge is in control of him/her or if he/she is in control of it.
Read books about my PRR's MH diagnosis. Seek counseling about what it could be like being in a RR with someone who has a particular MH challenge.	I will do the research before committing to a relationship with someone with a mental health challenge.	Being blindsided by unexpected behaviors that come with your PRR's mental health issue.
I will check any codependency issues of my own with a therapist to see if my empathy has led me to want to fix, rescue, save, and cure.	To be honest with myself about wanting to cure or "make better" someone else's challenges. If I discover those tendencies, I will back away from this romantic relationship.	I will enter a relationship without my eyes wide open with regard to my own unhealthy tendencies.

Mental Health Challenge Contract
for Already Established RRs

Agreements	My Responsibilities	Consequences for Breaking Agreements
We have discovered that you have a mental health challenge. I love you. I will learn all that I can about this diagnosis.	Go to the library, get counseling, call NAMI (National Alliance on Mental Illness) for more resources.	Not understanding your RR's diagnosis and how it affects behaviors.
I will assist you (if you want) in developing a protocol for dealing with your diagnosis. We will seek professional assistance to create this protocol.	I will set aside time dedicated to creating a supportive way to help you disallow your diagnosis from controlling your life.	Untreated and enabled mental health issues have a way of getting in the middle of a relationship.
We will write down the protocol and review it together.	Be creative, write down the protocol.	Without a protocol, mental health challenges can bring chaos into a RR because no one knows how to interact with the diagnosis.
I need you to delegate to me responsibilities for supporting you to follow your protocol when needed.	Write down my responsibilities as delegated by my RR.	Not knowing what to do when the problem takes over.

If you are considering a PRR, how do you know if a mental health challenge is driving his/her bus? Examine the chart below and use it as a measure with which to judge what tendencies are most evident.

Continuum of Mental Health and Well-Being

Mentally Unwell

Mental Health Issues

Mentally Healthy

Distressed

Poor coping skills

Hopelessness

Disconnected
from others

Angry outbursts

Sleeping too
much/little

Excessive anxiety
& worry

Pervasive sadness

Withdrawal

Resilient

Strong coping skills

Resourceful

Positive
relationships

Usual mood
fluctuations

Usual sleep patterns

Energized

Able to manage
challenges

Socially engaged

Cheating/Infidelity

There are so many examples of profoundly negative relationship consequences that are caused by infidelity. Just read *People* or watch *Entertainment Tonight*. Think about your own friends whose hearts have been broken by husband or wives cheating with best friends—or strangers. The situations are never-ending. The outcomes are always the same: suffering, anger, despair, and shock. Often, children are those who suffer the most.

I have watched people go through years of couple's counseling to no avail because the relationship victim has been unable to forgive and/or move on and the cheater doesn't do what is necessary to establish a "repair foundation" in the relationship. I have seen finances be the main reason people stay in what has become an unloving relationship. Unconsciously, and sometimes consciously, the person who has been cheated on often gets pleasure in making the cheater suffer. In monogamous relationships, cheating is a travesty. Even in open relationships, serial cheating often becomes painful for one member of the couple. As someone who is reading this book with an eye to keeping yourself out of unhappy romantic relationships, it will be necessary to learn the "cheating" history of your PRR. If you are in a committed RR, use your own judgment about whether or not this information would be beneficial to the relationship.

Learning the cheating history of your PRR can be very painful because:

1. It could bring up information that would lead you to end your RR. Your courage will be challenged.

2. It forces you to face values about infidelity, honesty, intimacy, love, trustworthiness, friendship, family, and dependability. If these are indeed some of your uncompromisable values, are you willing to ignore them for a PRR with a history of cheating? Are you willing to suffer? The Are You a Cheater? Interview forces us to face our own truth!

3. The "soft bed of denial" beckons us to get in and pull the covers over our heads and become comfortable with the belief, "I am different." "He/she would never do that to me." "This time it is different." "He/she will change." Denial allows us to create a belief system that ignores history, and it provides us with a relationship foundation supported by fantasy and tales that are based on our *wishes*! It is agonizing to get out of our goose-feathered bed of denial.

How does one ask a PRR about their cheating history? It is certainly *not* first-date material. However, the moment your PRR becomes an object of your affection, that is time to conduct the Are You a Cheater? Interview!

The Anatomy of Infidelity

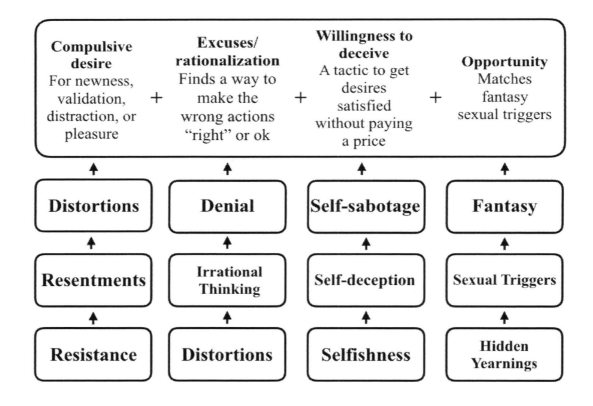

The Are You a Cheater? Interview

Have you ever been in a relationship in which you cheated on your partner/wife/husband, etc.?

If "no," you're done with this interview.

If "yes," here are the follow up questions:

    a) About how many relationships have you been in that you found yourself cheating?

    b) What was the situation?

    c) Why did you cheat?

    d) Could you have worked it out?

    e) Is it difficult for you to be in a steady relationship? Do you get bored?

    f) Do you consider sexual intercourse as being the only behavior that you define as cheating?

Put these questions in words that are comfortable for you. You do not have to ask every question on the interview. Sometimes the responses to just a few questions will give you more than enough information.

Juan and Abby

Abby is a 22-year-old high school graduate who has a history of selecting men that cheated on her in various ways. She has felt so heartbroken and depressed each time a partner cheats on her that she has lost faith that there is "a man out there who doesn't cheat." She sought therapy because she was "sick and tired of being taken advantage of and being lied to."

Abby participated in therapy for a few months. She completed the worksheets in this book and did a Value Sort. She felt she was now armed with tools to resist another relationship that was "based on lies." Then Abby met Juan, a 25-year-old whom she described as being as "handsome as my favorite singer, Bruno Mars." Abby was very infatuated with Juan. He treated her "like a queen" and took her out to fancy dinners, the movies, and to pricey bars. Abby informed her therapist that she was "paralyzed" by the thought of having to do the "Are You a Cheater? Interview" because "What if Juan doesn't like the questions? What if he doesn't want to take me out anymore because I asked him about his past with women?" Abby struggled with the idea of respecting her values and taking actions to honor them so she wouldn't suffer if it turned out that Juan was a "player."

It was pointed out to Abby that she was *not* asking about Juan's past with women, but rather about his history with being faithful while in a relationship. We discussed that if Abby got into a relationship with Juan, and if he had a history of infidelity, the odds would be that she would end up suffering from the violation of her values—having a trustworthy, faithful, and honest mate. Abby was in the limerence stages of her relationship with Juan, so the idea of exploring some areas where perhaps she and Juan didn't match was not something she wanted to do. But, being a brave woman, she did it!

ABBY: Oh Juan, I really love this restaurant. The food is delicious.

JUAN: Anything for you, Abby. I'm glad you like it. It makes me smile to have you happy.

ABBY (tempted to abandon her Are You a Cheater? Interview and just wallow in Juan's lovely words): That is so kind of you, Juan. I bet you are just naturally nice to women.

JUAN: Only when I am obsessed with them.

(**Red Flag**–limerence, "the love cocktail," the statement that he has a history of being "obsessed with a woman," that he treats a woman really well when he is obsessed, and the possibility that he has a "silver tongue" and uses flattery for some unknown reason *could* mean that Juan is just a really nice guy and is very attracted to Abby, but it could also suggest that Juan is a "player." Juan and Abby have only known each other four weeks.)

ABBY: I was wondering, Juan, have you ever been married?

JUAN: No, but if the right girl came along, I might consider it! (Giving a meaningful look at Abby to suggest that *she might be the one!*)

ABBY: Have you ever been in a serious relationship?

JUAN (staring at Abby in a way that makes her uncomfortable): Yes. What are you getting at?

ABBY (taking a huge breath): Well, we've been seeing each other for about a month, and I really enjoy your company. When I get to know someone who I might like to get to know better than just a casual friendship, I like to know a little more about them. Do you have any hesitation about us getting to know each other a little better?

JUAN: Of course not, Abby. What do you want to know?

ABBY (knowing she needs to finesse this well): I have had two past relationships that didn't work out. I think it is because those two guys and I had such different values. How long were your serious relationships?

JUAN: I had one serious relationship that lasted for three years.

ABBY: When did it end?

JUAN: About a month ago. (**RED FLAG**–that is just about the time Abby met Juan on an online dating site.)

ABBY: So am I the first one you have dated after the relationship breakup?

JUAN: Pretty much. I met you and really wasn't interested in looking further. (**RED FLAG!**–Juan doesn't even know Abby very well. Does he quickly move from one woman to another?)

ABBY: Why did you and your ex break up?

JUAN: She just sat around the apartment all day doing nothing. I have a kid with her and we don't agree on how to raise her. I couldn't stand watching her let the kid do anything she wanted.

ABBY: How old is your child?

JUAN: Three.

ABBY: So what happened?

JUAN: She accused me of cheating.

ABBY: Were you?

JUAN (getting defensive): Look, I have lots of women friends and I enjoy their company. She was jealous and wanted me to stay home all the time. She wanted me to give up anything in my life that was fun just to stay home with her. So I left! (**RED FLAG, RED FLAG, RED FLAG!**) She even hated my guy friends just because they wanted to come over to the apartment and watch sports on my 75-inch TV! I felt smothered. (**RED FLAG, RED FLAG, RED FLAG!**)

ABBY (slowly digesting all this information): That must have been really hard. (Great response!)

JUAN (said in a very bitter manner): It was, man. I can't even begin to tell you.

ABBY: Where do you live now?

JUAN: In the same apartment. She moved in with her parents and took the kid with her.

ABBY (changing the subject because she has more than enough information to work with on her Value Sort): Well, Juan, I can see this topic upsets you a little, so why don't we talk about something else? What sports teams do you like?

Abby did an excellent job. She has more than enough information with which to determine if Juan is a match for her. What did we find out about Juan?

1. He took *no* ownership of the problems in his relationship.
2. He did not discuss any attempts to collaborate or problem-solve with his ex. He reportedly left the relationship because of *her* behavior.
3. Juan appears to be more interested in being with his friends (female and male) than in staying home with his child and his baby's mother.

4. Juan has had one serious relationship in his 25 years. Abby might want to explore this more.
5. Juan seems to get defensive and aggressive when he is faced with uncomfortable questions.

Abby has enough information to decide if she wants a relationship with a man who, by his own self-report, doesn't take ownership of any behaviors that could have caused problems with his ex, whose primary interest is hanging out with his pals, and who gets defensive and aggressive when asked difficult questions.

The Fork in the Road

HERE WE ARE AT THE FORK IN THE ROAD!

The Left Fork

Abby could tell herself that she and Juan have a "special" relationship and nothing that happened in his past will be repeated when they are together. She could allow herself to ruminate on, *He is so handsome and sexy, I just can't resist him.*

The Right Fork

Abby could tell herself, "I need to sort out my values—I want fidelity, loyalty, a person who can work through problems with me and not just leave to avoid them. I want a man who takes an interest in his children."

We each come to this so-called "fork in the road." Investigate what goes into your left and right fork. Here's how:

The **left fork in the road** (LEAVE THE SCENE) and
the **right fork in the road** (STAY A WHILE AND SEE WHAT HAPPENS) inventory

When making a decision about a potential romantic relationship do I:

1. Let my emotions rule? (**left fork**)
☐ Yes
☐ No

2. Know what my *red flags* are? (**right fork**)
(Review your Value Sort—when those PRRs you are considering don't hold your same *uncompromisable* values—those are your *red flags*!)
☐ Yes
☐ No

3. Ignore *red flags*? (**left fork**)
☐ Yes
☐ No

4. Let myself continue to date a person who doesn't hold my same *uncompromisable* values because I don't want to hurt his/her feelings? or because he/she is so interesting?—whatever rationalization you want to use? (**left fork**)
☐ Yes
☐ No

5. Give a pass to the PRR when he/she hurts my feelings? Or violates my values? (**left fork**)
☐ Yes
☐ No

6. Place finances, looks, car, physique, bust size, etc., in the first line of decision-making when I am considering deepening my PRR? (If these things are your primary criteria when making a PRR decision: **left fork**.)
☐ Yes
☐ No

7. Not set boundaries with my PRR for fear he/she will leave me? (**left fork**)
☐ Yes
☐ No

8. Use great sex as the primary criteria for staying with a PRR? (**left fork**)
☐ Yes
☐ No

9. Leave a PRR when our uncompromisable values are not a match? (**right fork**)
☐ Yes
☐ No

10. Let my fears of being alone drive my decisions? (**left fork**)
☐ Yes
☐ No

Left Fork   **Right Fork**

Yeses _____   Yeses _____

Add up the left- and right-fork "Yes" answers.

What road are you following? If you are hanging out in the **left fork** in the road—you are almost guaranteed to have an unhappy romantic relationship.

Abby wanted to let her feelings toward Juan rule. After all, he was "so mysterious" and handsome and he drove a Corvette. Abby thought Juan had "so much potential!" ("Potential" is about *career*, not *character*.)

Then Abby looked at her Left and Right Fork in the Road Inventory and decided that she didn't want to go through all the pain that a relationship with Juan would probably bring with it. On the other hand, her heart wanted to stay with Juan because she liked him so much—she liked the *concept* of him. She didn't really know him well enough to like the person who Juan was. With much angst, grief, and with a very heavy heart, Abby pulled away—she took the **right fork** in the road.

A month later, Abby met Juan's sister, Nellie, by coincidence. To help her sad heart, and to get her mind off Juan, Abby had joined a hiking group. Of course at first Abby didn't know that her new acquaintance was Juan's sister. Nellie was a humorous 23-year-old. She kept her hiking group laughing by making jokes about her family and putting a funny spin on events that had happened to her. Nellie shared about "what a player my brother is," as she told the group about a flat tire he had on the freeway during a first date "with another of his endless line of bimbos." Abby was silent when Nellie described her brother as "Juan, the dude who looks like Bruno Mars, but he's not Mars or Venus or even Neptune. He's more like the Sun—bringing light to all but full of gas!" There it was! Validation for Abby's decision.

Yes, there was still some sadness for Abby. She didn't have dates with Juan to dream about. She couldn't hang out in a "living fantasy" about being Juan's girlfriend. She was grateful for hearing what Nellie said on the hike. She got through it. A year later Abby met a man who was a match for most (not everyone is a perfect) of her uncompromisable values. Today, Abby's PRR is a committed relationship and is so happy that she didn't remain as one of the planets circling the Sun.

Infidelity Contract

Agreement	My Responsibilities	Consequences for Breaking Agreements
I want to be with a person who is loyal to our relationship and who holds the value of monogamy.	To have a conversation about this value with my PRR.	Not knowing if you and your PRR hold the same value regarding fidelity.
Because I am committed to respecting this value I will conduct the "Are You a Cheater?" Interview with all my PRRs.	To address how my PRR feels about cheating while in a committed relationship.	Not doing your research in this area could land you with a person who does not value monogamy in his/her relationships. This will cause you suffering.
I will not tell myself that "I am special" or that "This relationship will be different" if my PRR has a history of cheating in committed relationships.	To believe that relationship history usually repeats itself unless people have made a concerted effort to change and have in fact, made the changes, and can tell you what changes they have made.	Entering into denial about how another person's relationship behaviors will change because now he/she is in a relationship with *you*!
If I have a history of infidelity and have violated my own value in the past, I will seek help for learning how to adjust my behavior so I will not continue to violate my own romantic relationship values.	To seek council from a professional person about what I need to do to change my behavior so I will honor my fidelity and other RR values. I will work to make the necessary changes by following their feedback.	Continuing to violate your values about fidelity in a committed relationship.

Narcissism

What is narcissism? It is self-absorption, self-admiration, conceit, vanity, extreme selfishness, a grandiose view of one's own talents, self-centeredness, and a deep need for admiration. These traits are accompanied by lack of empathy for others and a propensity to be aggressive and defensive at the slightest criticism.

If you have ever been in a relationship where there is no *you*, you have been with a narcissist. If you have ever been in a relationship in which the only opinion that matters is the other person's, then you've been with a narcissist.

In her article, "Are You a Narcissist? Six Sure Signs of Narcissism,"[16] Dr. Susan Heitler identified traits that indicate you are with a narcissist:

1. Unilateral listening—what I want and what I have to say are all that matters when we talk together. When we discuss issues, my opinions are right. If you disagree or expect to have input, you are undermining me.
2. It's all about *me*—I know more, I know better, I'm more interesting, and I get to take up most of the air time. If you talk about yourself, I bring it back to me.
3. The rules don't apply to *me*—rules are for other people to follow; I can cheat on you, on my taxes, and even cut in line in front of others.
4. Your concerns are really criticisms of me, and I hate being criticized—I hear your concerns as disguised ways of criticizing me. I can criticize others (and often do) but if you criticize me, you hurt my feelings, and your feelings must be all about what I have been doing.
5. I'm right. You're wrong. So when things go wrong between us, it's always your fault—I can't be expected to apologize or to admit blame because I am above reproach. If you expect me to say how I've contributed to a problem, I'll get mad at you.
6. I may be quick to anger but when I get angry, it's because *you*...—if I'm mad, it's because I'm frustrated by what you are doing. My anger is your fault. I'm only mad because you…

If you are with a narcissist, you are in a relationship that will ensure suffering because you literally, don't matter.

---

[16] *https://www.psychologytoday.com/us/blog/resolution-not-conflict/201210/are-you-narcissist-6-sure-signs-narcissism*

Narcissists violate almost every value in the Value Sort except maybe, contribution (they are often very successful business people), achievement (they are usually able to realize their non–RR goals), and power (to have control over others).

Contract for Being Valued in a
Romantic Relationship

Agreement	My Responsibilities	Consequences for Breaking Agreements
Now that I know about narcissism, I will listen for narcissistic traits in my PRR and in my RR.	To determine if there is a *you* in your PRR or RR.	Staying in a relationship or getting into a relationship in which you are not valued because there is *no you*!
Review the narcissistic traits listed above and determine if you are in a relationship with a narcissist.	Be truthful with yourself and don't rationalize or excuse the outcome from your review.	Ignoring why you feel unvalued, unheard, defensive, stupid, wrong, criticized, and not good enough when interacting with your PRR or RR. Continuing to feel discounted.
I will review my Value Sort.	Determine how many of my values are being overridden and discounted by my PRR or RR.	Suffering because you allow your PRR or RR to disrespect your values. You disrespect your values.
Narcissism is part of one's character. I will acknowledge that I am unable to change my PRR or RR by discussing how I feel.	To take to heart the saying, "When people show you who they are, believe them."	Continue in a subservient, "not good enough" position in your PRR or RR.

Hiding Your Authentic Self

What is the "authentic self"? Dr. Phil provides us with a definition that touches the heart. He says, "The authentic self is the you that can be found at your absolute core. It is the part of you not defined by your job function, or role."[17] Judy Garland provided an insight by noting, "Be a first-rate version of yourself, not a second-rate version of someone else."

The way to find one's authentic self is by knowing one's values. It is realized by comparing what you "do" in your life with what your values are.

The values you hold as uncompromisable equal your authentic self. The values you violate and how you violate them is how you hide your authentic self in relationships. In romantic relationships we usually violate our uncompromisable values by deferring to the wants of others; we hide our authentic self to get in and stay in a romantic relationship. Why doesn't this work in the long term? Because we suffer when we live a lie. We emotionally hurt and ache when we can't be our authentic selves. There cannot be emotional intimacy when we hide who we really are!

There is another element to hiding our authentic selves. I call this the "social mask syndrome." We enter this syndrome when we create so many different masks to hide our authentic self from our PRR or RR that we allow ourselves to get subsumed in the personality of the other person. When we allow this, we end up not knowing who we actually are. For example, there's the "I love sports" mask

---

[17] *http://www.drphil.com/advice/defining-your-authentic-self/.*

worn by someone who hates sports but pretends to like them to please his/her partner. There's the "I love to cook" mask worn by someone who either is too busy to cook or who doesn't like it. My recent favorite is the "I love going to the gym" mask often worn by a couch potato who has become interested in a buffed-out gym rat. The "I am whoever you want me to be" mask is the one that is often the most emotionally painful, because this mask extinguishes the authentic self.

Terry and Ellen

Terry met Ellen at a time when she held a part-time job as an usher at the symphony. Ellen hated the symphony. She preferred rap music and when she wasn't acting as an usher, she put her earbuds in so she wouldn't have to listen to the "boring" music being played on stage.

Terry, who was 10 years older than Ellen, was a devotee of classical music. His passion was to see and hear Bach or Mozart symphonies, Chopin concertos, and works by some of his other favorite composers. He owned a home that had been outfitted with surround sound so he could fill his house with the music he loved.

Terry frequented the symphony, and he and Ellen had developed a "hi, how are you" relationship because Ellen had made it a point to guide Terry to his seat every time he attended. Over time, Terry had begun asking Ellen personal questions such as, why she was working as an usher (answer: I'm finishing college and need extra money) and if she lived close to the concert hall (answer: yes, I live a few blocks away). Terry thought Ellen was "quite attractive" and he liked the way she looked.

One evening before the program started, Terry invited Ellen to coffee after the symphony. Ellen agreed and they met at the local coffeehouse. Terry's conversation was mostly about his love of classical music and how his home had surround sound so he could listen to it all the time. He asked Ellen what kind of music she liked, and before Ellen could respond Terry made the observation that she must love classical music because she chose to work at Symphony Hall.

Because Ellen thought Terry was a PRR, she enthused about that evening's symphony, and exclaimed how wonderful it must be for Terry to be surrounded by classical music all the time. In response to Ellen's inquiry, Terry told her he also specifically subscribed to Sirius so he could listen to the classics while he drove.

Ellen did not broach the topic of her love of rap music. She did not tell Terry that she loved to dance to Drake, Jay-Z, and Eminem. She did not share that she felt rap music touched her soul. This was the beginning of Ellen hiding her authentic self. She created an entirely new Ellen (let's call her "Ellie" so we can differentiate) when she was with Terry.

Ellie liked to dress up for the symphony, go to fancy restaurants, and was considering adding music classes to her college courses—Terry liked that.

Ellen liked miniskirts, going to rap concerts, eating fast food, being casual, going to the gym, and playing the drums—Terry didn't know that.

Over time, Ellen allowed her likes to be eradicated by Terry's because they became romantically involved and Ellen wanted to "keep Terry because he has a good job, is financially stable, and I dig his house." Ellen, wearing the Ellie mask, had purchased "traditional" clothing, had hidden her love of rap, and stopped going to the rap clubs with her college friends.

One year after their first coffee date, Terry invited Ellie to move in with him. Terry thought he had found the "woman of my dreams who shares my passion for classical music." Ellen had hidden who she really was from Terry. There could never be intimacy in this relationship because Terry was in a relationship with a stranger, and Ellen had been wearing her Ellie mask for so long she felt confused about what she liked and what she didn't like. She felt like a fraud. She *was* a fraud.

(So, reader, you could be saying to yourself, "Yeah, but we all do that about some stuff." I ask you, "Why?" Why do we hide our authentic selves? It leads to being "fake" in our romantic relationships. It brings unhappiness. And if we wear too many masks, we get confused and we confuse our partner.)

One day, Terry came home from work early. As he entered his front door he was blasted by Lil Wayne's song "Sucker for Pain." Terry stood in his front room as he listened to the unbelievable: rap music coming through his surround sound. He ran up the stairs to find Ellen.

There she was! In a very short miniskirt, dancing around the bedroom, keeping beat with the music. That was the beginning of Terry and Ellen's (aka Ellie's) downfall. Terry felt lied to, deceived, and used. There was no putting it back together.

Are you thinking that this relationship could have been put back together if the couple had just worked on it? Two of Terry's core values were honesty and responsibility. Two of Ellen's uncompromisable values were excitement and fun. Their relationship had been based on dishonesty and immaturity for Terry. Ellen found the relationship boring and tiring. It was a relationship built on sand. Ellen had hidden an important part of her authentic self from Terry. Any part of our authentic self that we hide from our RR will lead to suffering for us and our partner.

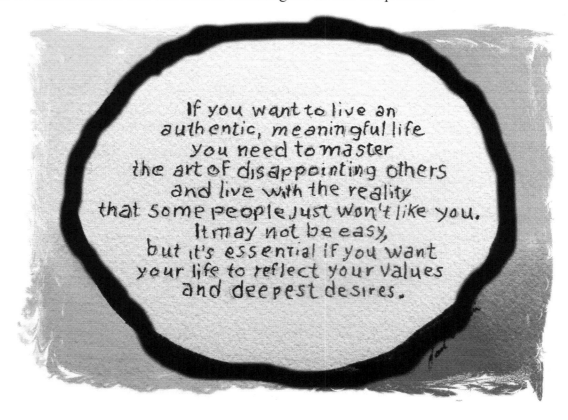

If you want to live an authentic, meaningful life you need to master the art of disappointing others and live with the reality that some people just won't like you. It may not be easy, but it's essential if you want your life to reflect your values and deepest desires.

Contract to Avoid Hiding
My Authentic Self

Agreement	My Responsibilities	Consequences for Breaking Agreements
I will honor my uncompromisable values and not hide them because my PRR or RR doesn't hold the same ones.	To be my *real* self in my romantic relationship.	Having your PRR fall in love with a fake, made-up person. Having your RR realize that you are NOT who you said you were. Suffering in both cases.
I will harness my fear(s) about a PRR not liking me because I don't agree with him/her.	To practice the principles of "Fair Fighting Rules" (in Chapter 4).	Deferring to your PRR or RR and staying in hiding.
I will learn about assertiveness and practice how to disagree in a kind manner.	To use "I" statements when expressing my thoughts, feelings, wants, needs.	If you don't tell your PRR or RR what you want, you will be disappointed with their inability to mind-read. You will remain in hiding your authentic self.
I will practice being my authentic self with safe people.	Being honest about my dreams, likes, dislikes, values, etc.	Suffering behind the mask you developed so people will like you—the false you!

Making a Commitment Against One's Better Judgment

Why would anyone ever make a commitment against one's better judgment? There are so many reasons we can't begin to address them. Here is a main reason that most of us haven't even heard about—*akrasia*! Yes, that's it! We make commitments against our better judgments because of akrasia![18]

The *akrasia effect* (from the Greek, "lacking control") is when we do one thing even though we know we should be doing something else. Procrastination is just one of the possible manifestations of akrasia. We procrastinate in following our values/intuitions and, before we know it, we find ourselves in committed RRs that we know are unhealthy, not a good match, irritating, etc. Often we don't actually make a commitment to our RR, we just fall into it.

The akrasia effect merits understanding because we humans are driven by it. The human brain focuses on immediate rewards more than it focuses on future payoffs. For example, even though we intuitively know that our current RR is a problematic alcoholic, our brain tells us that he/she is so much fun we continue to be with him/her because the occasion is more gratifying than focusing on what the future might be like with a person who is dependent on alcohol. This is known as "time inconsistency"—the brain's desire for immediate rewards rather than future ones.

We can label the act of making a commitment against one's better judgment by many different names: ignoring our intuition, rationalization, being a "chicken," "giving our RR another chance," etc., but it all boils down to akrasia.

As a postscript, the ability to delay gratification is a great predictor of happiness and life successes. If we don't learn how to delay gratification, it will be very difficult to avoid unhappy romantic relationships!

---

[18] James Clear, *"The Akrasia Effect: Why We Don't Follow Through on What We Set Out to Do and What to Do About It,"* http://jamesclear.com/akrasia.

Contract to Avoid Making a Commitment Against My Better Judgment

Agreement	My Responsibilities	Consequences for Breaking Agreements
When I am trying to decide about making a romantic commitment, I will do a "Ben Franklin" in which I list the pros and cons on paper.	To complete the "Ben Franklin" as demonstrated below.	Acting on emotion without weighing what your authentic self is telling you. Violating your values.
I will consider which of my values I would be violating if I entered into a RR with _____ (name).	To make a list of values I think I will be violating if I enter into a relationship with ____(name).	Violating your own values and therefore giving your PRR permission to do the same.
To be as honest with myself as I can be. If I am not, it will only cause suffering later.	To be honest with myself. To resist thinking that the person you are considering for a RR will change.	Allowing temporary emotions, oxytocin, and limerence to sabotage your judgment.
If the "Con" column in the "Ben Franklin" scale is above 2, I will not enter into a RR with _____ (name). If the Value Violations total is above 2, I will not enter into a relationship with _____ (name).	To move on and respect my values and intuition. I will participate in lots of activities with friends so as not to second-guess my intuition.	Suffering in sequential relationships. Disenabling yourself to find a good match.

An Example "Ben Franklin"
What my intuition tells me about Sue.

Pros about Sue:
- Good sex
- Makes good money
- Likes sports

Total: <u>3</u>

Cons about Sue:
- Clingy
- Wants to borrow money all the time
- Smokes pot
- Sloppy about her personal hygiene
- Bad breath
- Smokes cigarettes
- Her car's a mess
- Hates dogs
- Too opinionated

Total: <u>9</u>

What my heart tells me. (Things you are feeling.)
- She's really fun.
- I feel sad her father died recently.
- She's had a hard life and I could help her.
- I'm a good listener and she needs someone to be there for her.

What my intellect tells me. (Things you are thinking.)
- I'm not sure she's right for me.
- She comes from a dysfunctional family and will bring that into our relationship.
- I don't like her mother and I have noticed similar qualities in Sue.
- I don't like her occupation no matter how much money she is making.
- There is something wrong with someone who doesn't like dogs.

Value Violation

Ask Sue to do the Value Sort. This can be presented in a fun way. "In order to get to know you better, I'd like to know what you value. Will you do this Value Sort with me, and then we can compare?"

If you have more than two uncompromisable values that don't match, perhaps this is not the right relationship for you. Go back and review your cons.

There is no need to make an immediate decision, but the longer we stay in a PRR that our intuition tells us to be cautious about, the more likely it is that we will walk the path from limerence to suffering in an unhappy romantic relationship.

The Inability to Problem-Solve

Many of us in URRs (unhappy romantic relationships) find ourselves in the arguing-explaining-fighting-for-the-win dynamic that is repetitive, disrespectful, and vengeful. This dynamic never solves the problem we are arguing about.

There are some concepts we attach to arguing: the "win" and the idea of "losing." I ask patients, "What do you get when you win an argument? Is there a trophy that you are going after?" They often respond by saying that they get "satisfaction." They get to know they have "made my point."

To continue that line of questioning, I ask, "What do you get when you lose an argument? Do people boo you when you leave the local supermarket?" The most frequent answer is, "I don't know."

Winning an argument is a lose-lose for all participants. The person who "wins" often feels smug and superior whereas the person who "loses" often feels they have been so humiliated and demeaned that they just give up. Note, *there is no problem-solving. There is no collaboration to find a solution.*

Dr. Stephen Karpman developed what he named the "drama triangle" to describe the relationships in which there is no problem-solving.[19] He conceptualized three roles—the victim, the persecutor, and the rescuer. To simplify his theory, the victim is the one who "loses" and the person who is "not OK." The persecutor is the person who attacks the victim in order to "win." The persecutor "is OK." The rescuer is the one who tries to put things back together and reinstate the status quo. These roles are not static; they are interchangeable so the "persecutor" can also become the "victim," or the "rescuer" as can the rescuer and victim take on the other roles. The roles can change within a single argument! People who find themselves in this type of unhealthy romantic relationship repetitively relive drama with no end in sight.

---

[19] *Stephen B. Karpman, MD, A Game Free Life (Drama Triangle Publications, 2015), https://www.karpmandramatriangle.com.*

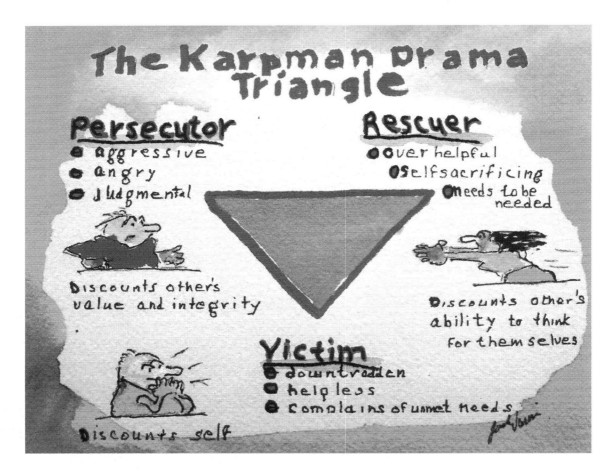

Unsolved problems build up to resentments. They can evolve into deep emotional wounds. Unsolved issues pile up until there are so many that the RR seems hopeless. It feels like we are caught in a spiderweb with no way out. We simply spin and spin. We suffer. And nothing changes.

Tina and Louise

Tina and Louise had been in a romantic relationship for three years. A recurring issue between them was that Tina liked to spend money, and Louise was financially conservative and preferred to save money for her retirement.

> LOUISE (yelling): Tina! Look at this Visa bill! Just how could you spend $400 at the bookstore? We don't have that kind of money! I am sick and tired of this! This just pisses me off because you never pay for your expenses. All you do is cry and whine until I pay it. (*PERSECUTOR*)
>
> TINA: I'm so sorry. I couldn't help it. I thought if I got some books on budgeting I could better manage my spending. You always me make me feel so stupid—even when I'm trying to do better. I can't believe you are so mean. (*VICTIM*)
>
> LOUISE: OK. I didn't know it was for books about financial planning. I guess I'll pay for it— *again*. (*RESCUER*)

TINA: I am sick of you yelling at me all the time. You are always so angry. You make me sick! (*PERSECUTOR*)

LOUISE (dejected): I apologize. It's just that all your spending is not leaving any money to put toward my retirement, and you know how important that is to me. I can't do both. I just don't know what to do. (*VICTIM*)

Louise and Tina haven't solved this issue; they keep doing the same interaction over and over—it's the never-ending drama triangle!

Contract to Avoid Being with a
Partner Who Won't Solve Problems

Agreement	My Responsibilities	Consequences for Breaking Agreements
There is no benefit in arguing with a PRR or a RR. My goal is collaboration and problem-solving.	To discuss with your PRR how they solve problems. Discuss with your RR how you would like to stop arguing and move on to problem-solving.	Being stuck in arguments that won't solve any problem.
I will role play problem-solving with a trusted friend.	To select a subject for your argument. Role play arguing then role play problem-solving.	Reliving the same argument with no end.
Practice your new problem-solving techniques with your PRR or RR.	To watch to see if your new problem-solving techniques lead to the desired result.	Staying in a relationship in which there is just drama and no collaboration.
With a PRR, determine whether you are considering someone who is incapable of solving problems. With a RR, determine if this is the type of relationship you want.	Remember, if *you* don't change the problem-solving dynamics in your PRRs or RRs, no one will.	Being stuck in the problem… over and over and over again!

How to Solve a Problem

First of all, get out of the drama triangle if you have identified that this is your problem-solving dynamic. Then work on making changes so that there is collaboration and focus on the goal—solving the issue. Set up some ground rules for problem-solving, such as:

- Make an appointment with your partner.
- Agree to not call names, raise your voice—going to a public place helps if you and your RR have communication challenges during differences of opinion.
- Set up some agreements: discuss only one topic, don't interrupt, use "I" statements, stay away from demeaning, name calling, etc.
- Pay attention. Don't check your cell phone, allow yourself to become distracted, change the topic.
- Don't blame.
- Own your part in the problem.
- Be open to solution options other than your own.

After setting guidelines, then get down to the business of solving your problem:

- Define your problem.
- Talk and *listen*.
- Write down the definition of the problem and agree on it.
- Decide on a plan.
- Evaluate your solution.
- Say what you like (be authentic) and speak for yourself in a respectful way.
- Try your solution.
- Reevaluate.

Problem solved?
☐ Yes. Move on to the next issue.
☐ No. Repeat the steps above.

In couples' problem-solving, if there is an agreement that your partner doesn't follow, then it is time to evaluate if you are in a relationship with a person whose word you can count on. If not, one or more of your values is being violated. Are you in a URR in which there is *no* problem-solving? Be honest with yourself and sort out your options.

Codependency

Codependency is too a huge topic to completely cover in this section. There are many books on this subject. Suffice it to say, that if *you* are a codependent, chances are that you will find yourself in URRs because *your* happiness depends on whether your partner is doing what you want; your happiness depends on *something outside yourself.* I have *never* seen codependence produce happiness. Why? Because codependence is actually a control issue.

While codependents think they are helpful, giving, and kind, their helpfulness, benevolence, and kindness has strings attached. What might those strings be? Appreciation, gratitude, and compliance! We codependents want to be thanked for our "help" (which translates to "control"). We feel devastated when the people we help don't follow our advice.

In the area of romance, codependents take on "projects." They select emotionally needy others to save, rescue, lecture to, and often emotionally punish when their guidance is not followed. Codependency creates unfulfilling power struggles in RRs.

Amelia and Lester

Amelia and Lester were in their thirties and had been married two years when they came for counseling regarding Amelia's unwillingness to stop gambling. Before they married, they used to have great fun playing blackjack at the local casino, but now that they were married, Lester had become concerned about how much Amelia was losing at the card table.

Amelia had gambled away $10,000 at the casino, and Lester had paid her debt (RESCUING). He had expected Amelia to be grateful and change her ways, but Amelia continued to gamble and charge her losses to her Visa card. She didn't thank Lester for paying off her debt (well, maybe once), and she didn't listen to his lectures about getting help for her addiction. Just the suggestion that she had a gambling problem evoked such rages that Lester had grown tired of listening to her screaming and name calling, and had taken up woodworking in the garage to avoid her.

Lester believed that *if only* Amelia would get help and stop gambling, he would be happy, and they would have a happy marriage. The third year of their marriage consisted of Amelia incurring more gambling debt, Lester bailing her out, and both of them arguing about her problem, and his disappointment that he couldn't help her and she wouldn't listen to him (let him control her).

The truth was that Amelia didn't want to stop gambling and didn't want help for her addiction. Lester, who would not take "no" for an answer, believed that he could cajole, lecture, and somehow convince her to "see the light" and change her ways. What had started out as a kind, loving, and fun RR, evolved into a power struggle: Amelia's gambling and Lester's attempts to change (control) her.

Codependency causes suffering for the codependent because he/she is not being allowed to control the situation he/she doesn't like. Suffering leads to URRs. Codependency causes great unhappiness for the "identified patient" (IP) because he/she wants freedom to be him/herself and *not* the advice, lectures, and control forced on him/her by the codependent. The IP's primary relationship is often with the behavior the codependent wants to change, and the codependent wants to be the primary relationship—the person the IP turns to for advice and guidance.

We can't control people, places, or things. We only have charge of ourselves. Control leads to URRs—without exception.

Now go to the worksheet titled "The 'Most Likely Causes of My Unhappy Romantic Relationships' Worksheet," below, to determine which of the listed categories have most likely been the cause of your unhappy romantic relationships. These are the areas in which you need to work on change.

The "Most Likely Causes of My Unhappy Romantic Relationships" Worksheet

1. Have you ever been in a relationship in which you ignored the offensive behaviors or character traits of your boyfriend/girlfriend?

☐ Yes
☐ No

If you checked "Yes," working on identifying your values and being dedicated to *not violating them* will assist you in overcoming the tendency to overlook behaviors in a PRR that irritate you. Over time, those characteristics will increasingly annoy you and cause you suffering, because in some way they violate your values.

Partial list of behaviors many have reported that they find annoying (add your own to this list):
- Bad table manners | VV (value violation): courtesy
- Poor driving | VV: safety
- Leaving the housework to *you* | VV: cooperation, fairness, caring
- Picking up | VV: justice, order, cooperation
- Inability to organize | VV: order
- Poor grammar | VV: knowledge, education, mastery
- Swearing | VV: politeness, courtesy, self-control
- Arguing politics | VV: justice, tradition, safety.

People are entitled to be whoever they want to be and do whatever they want to do, but if you find who they are and what they do irritating and give a pass to those traits that exasperate you, you will be in an unhappy romantic relationship and the "romantic" part will eventually fade away.

2. Have you ever been in a relationship with a person who has substance abuse or behavioral addiction issues?

☐ Yes
☐ No

If you checked "Yes," your work will be to believe that *you can never be in a satisfying romantic relationship* with someone who is addicted to drugs/alcohol or gambling, sex, shopping, eating, etc. The reason is that the addict's first love and primary relationship is with the substance or addictive behavior. This will always come first. *You will not come first!* Trying to wedge one's way between an addict and the object of his/her addiction never works. Thinking that *you* can "help" the addict who does not want to change is an illusion.

Consider if you want to be in a RR in which your participation in your partner's addiction is the main organizing principle of the relationship.

Partial list of lies we tell ourselves about why getting involved with a PRR or staying in a RR with a person who has an active addiction will be satisfying:

- This is really fun! I love to gamble, eat, smoke pot, go to bars. We won't do this forever. (With an addict, *yes you will!*) VV: balance, order, intimacy
- Once we are committed to each other, things will change—his/her priorities will change. (*No they won't.*) VV: intimacy, inner peace, romance
- It's not really that bad. (If you have noticed that your PRR or RR is focused on drinking, using, gambling, eating, etc., *it really is that bad*.) VV: honesty, balance, comfort, commitment

3. Have you ever been in a RR with someone who lets their untreated mental health challenges control the relationship?

☐ Yes
☐ No

If you checked "Yes," your work will be to conduct a thorough PRR interview so you will know the mental health history of your PRR and learn what they have done or not done to diminish the control of their mental health challenges over the course of their life.

Having depression, anxiety, bipolar disorder, ADHD, and other common mental health challenges determines what happens in your RR and can cause suffering and feelings of powerlessness. Remember, most mental health issues can be treated behaviorally and/or with medications. If you find yourself considering or already with someone who doesn't want treatment, review your values and consider which ones you will be violating. Some VV possibilities are: independence, inner peace, intimacy, order, pleasure, responsibility, simplicity, solitude.

Remember, people who have mental health challenges are not responsible for having them, but they *are* responsible for managing them.

4. Have you ever been in a RR with someone who has cheated on you?

☐ Yes

☐ No

5. Do you have a history of cheating while in a committed relationship?

☐ Yes

☐ No

If you checked "Yes," to either or both of the questions above, your work will be threefold:

a. Write down what your feelings were when you found out that your partner cheated on you or when your partner found out that you cheated on him/her. Do you want to feel like this again?

☐ Yes

☐ No

b. Were you able to repair your relationship? What did you do to repair it? Write those efforts down. Continue to do the behaviors that helped you repair your RR. Repair work is *never* completed.

Things I did to successfully repair infidelity in my RR:

| |
| |
| |
| |
| |
| |
| |
| |
| |

c. Answer these questions:

6. Did you have any part in creating a relationship in which you or your partner succumbed to the lure of physical/emotional intimacy outside your relationship?

☐ Yes

☐ No

What was *your* part? (You could take your partner's inventory, but you have no control over what your partner does—you only have control over yourself, so it is not worthwhile to ruminate on how you were the victim.)

Here are some ideas to consider about your part in a RR that has infidelity in it. You:

- Became emotionally distant or selected someone who was emotionally distant, thinking you could change that person.
- Withheld or were not interested in sex, or selected someone who was not interested in physical intimacy.
- Didn't listen to your partner, or selected someone who didn't listen to you.
- Blamed your partner for all the unhappiness in your relationship, or selected someone who blamed you for every malfunction.
- Ignored your partner's history of infidelity, or didn't change your tendency to cheat while in a committed romantic relationship.
- Thought your understanding and compassionate personality would change your partner or thought your PRR's compassionate and understanding personality would change you.

This is *your* inventory to do. If you don't do this work, everything you did in your current/past relationship will replay itself in a different one. In no way is this inventory meant to infer that *you* were the cause of your partner's infidelity (emotionally or physically), but let's face it, people in a happy romantic relationship don't tend to cheat on their partner. This inventory is actually about *you* not doing your value homework when you selected a RR. VV: to be loved, monogamy, openness, responsibility, respect, romance, sexuality, virtue, comfort, commitment, dependability, faithfulness, family, friendship, honesty.

Further work: always do the Are You a Cheater? Interview *before* you even entertain getting into a RR. **Note:** People who have been divorced or separated are twice as likely to cheat, so the relationship history is very important. Look at the statistics below:[20]

---

[20] Susan Walsh, "Everything You Always Wanted to Know About Infidelity But Were Afraid to Ask," *Hooking Up Smart* (July 24, 2013). *http://www.hookingupsmart.com/2013/07/24/relationshipstrategies/the-definitive-survey-of-infidelity-in-marriage-and-relationships/.*

For men it's 28% vs. 14%:

Have Had Sex With Other Than Spouse While Married, By Respondent's Gender

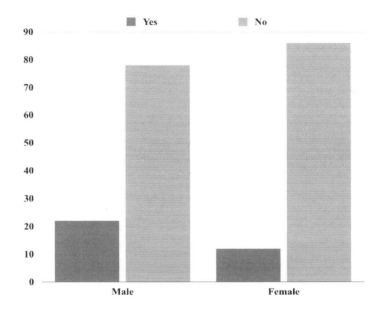

And for women it's 19% vs. 7%:

Have Had Sex With Other Than Spouse While Married, By "Ever Been Divorced or Separated?"

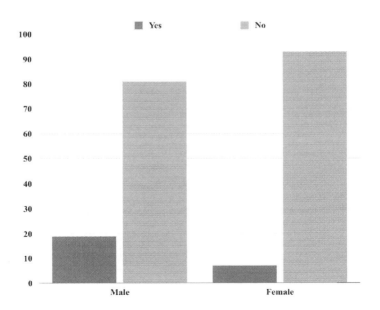

Remember, people with a history of cheating while in a committed relationship can change, but it is doubtful they will if they don't get help from their counselor, pastor, relationship classes, therapist, etc.

7. Have you ever been in a RR in which your partner did not consider your feelings or goals; instead he/she criticized and blamed you for outcomes that were not your fault? The question here really is, "Have you ever been in a relationship with a narcissist?"

☐ Yes
☐ No

Those of us who have grown up in families in which one or more of the adults is a narcissist tend to select narcissists as partners because the relationship feels so familiar. We victims of narcissists spend our life trying to get validation, recognition, compassion, understanding, and positive mirroring—to no avail.

Review the six signs that are indications you are with a narcissist (in the "Narcissism" section of Chapter 3). Review them again and again. When you are considering a PRR, look for these signs. Then *run* if you find more than one. If you are already in a URR with a narcissist your work is:

a. Finding another person/people to use as a mirror to how *you* are, how you are doing, and as a positive reinforcement for your accomplishments.

b. Reviewing your values to determine which ones you have allowed your narcissist to violate. You can turn this around with assertiveness and by knowing what *you* want.

Example of an Assertiveness Intervention

I want you to know that I feel sad when you blame me for _____ and I want you to stop. I *value* (name your value) _____, not blame. (That is all you have to say—leave the room—this is not a discussion; it is simply a statement! This is not a plea for your narcissist to change, because when someone is "perfect" there is no need to change! This is a way to acknowledge critical behavior!)

VV: acceptance, adaptability, balance, caring, comfort, compassion, courtesy, fairness, love, nurturance, respect, safety, tolerance… to name a few.

Remember, if you are with a narcissist, *there is no you*!

8. Have you ever been in a relationship in which you felt the need to conceal your true self?
☐ Yes
☐ No

Low self-esteem, dependency needs, and shame are often the reasons people try to hide who they *really* are when it comes to a romantic relationship. Disallowing one's self to be original and genuine in a PRR or RR is like wearing Halloween costumes or masks throughout one's day-to-day life.

It is exhausting, and it causes suffering because we can never relax—we are in hiding from perceived judgments.

What are perceived judgments? They are made-up stories that we tell ourselves about the negative thoughts we think someone is having, or will have, about us if we are authentic. For example, someone might be afraid of letting a PRR who is an avid follower of politics know that he/she loathes the entire subject and couldn't care less. That person might fear that the PRR would think they are too stupid and dreary to even understand politics and want to leave the potential romantic relationship. In other words, we tell ourselves stories that undermine who we really are for fear of nonacceptance.

Your work in this area is to learn what your values are, and to respect them. Your work in this area is to let go of making up stories about how someone else would not like you if they really knew you.

Low self-esteem comes from thinking there is something innately wrong with you. Figure out what is *right* with you. Direct your thoughts toward that.

Dependency needs are about feeling weak, incompetent, and powerless. These judgment perceptions can lead to looking for someone else to take care of you and relieve you from self-care responsibilities. Write down what your self-care duties are; practice being responsible for tending to your needs. (Dialectical behavior therapy is a great treatment for dependency needs.)

Shame is a very deep topic that is not going to be addressed in a comprehensive manner here. Let's look at shame as the feelings of guilt that arise when one's internal values aren't respected. Shame arises when one's imagined or real defects are exposed to others. Write down your uncompromisable values. Your defects of character arise and you feel shamed when you violate your values. Being your "inauthentic" self by hiding who you genuinely are only creates more shame because *you* are violating/disrespecting your true character and fear someone will find out! Practice honoring your values by not compromising in romantic relationships.

Making a Commitment Against One's Better Judgment

9. Have you ever agreed to be in a committed romantic relationship when you knew you should not?
☐ Yes
☐ No

10. Have you ever stayed in a committed romantic relationship when you knew you should leave?
☐ Yes
☐ No

When we make a commitment against our better judgment, we immediately violate our uncompromisable values.

The Inability to Problem-Solve

11. Have you ever been in a committed romantic relationship in which you and your partner were unable to solve problems?
☐ Yes
☐ No

Inability to find solutions to differences between partners becomes a foundation for arguments, dashed expectations, and resentment.

Codependency

12. Have you ever been in a committed romantic relationship in which you have given unsolicited advice or tried to save, fix, rescue, or change your partner?
☐ Yes
☐ No

When we attempt to control relationships by putting ourselves in a position of superiority and our partner in a position of inferiority, our partnership becomes more of a parent/child exercise. Is that what you want?

Add up the total "Yeses." _____

For items that received a "Yes," these are the areas in which *you* seed your very own unhappy romantic relationship(s). These items are some of the most powerful disruptors of romantic relationships. If you have checked "Yes" to more than three of the areas listed above, you might consider taking a "relationship vacation," until you can get some help with and perspective on your propensity to select people who will cause you to suffer. Additionally, if you select PRRs or stay in RRs in which *you* are the one who seeds suffering for your partner, counseling will assist you in rooting out the causes for selecting "victims," and assist you in changing your selection criteria.

Assertiveness

First rule: *don't start sentences with the word "you"!* Starting a sentence with "you" only puts the receiver on the defensive. Here is the "assertiveness script." Practice it and incorporate it into your romantic relationship. Assertiveness will help you define how you feel and what you want. It will help you in becoming authentic and honest with others.

I feel _____
(*insert a feeling word here*)

sad	mad	glad	scared
hurt	disappointed	joyous	lost
betrayed	angry	happy	frightened
anguished	frustrated	delighted	lonely
discouraged	irritated	confident	confused
embarrassed	annoyed	accepting	worried
numb	provoked	satisfied	nervous
powerless	resentful	thankful	suspicious

when you _____
(*list a specific behavior or two, not a laundry list, and* not *something like "you act like a jerk," or "you treat me badly"*)

because _____
(*a brief explanation of the effect on you; not a justification of bad reactive behavior*)

Then ask for what you need/want:
Are you able to _____?

For example:
I **feel** hurt **when you** are late for dinner **because** I value this time when we are together as a family.
Are you able to leave work at a regular time?

Contract to Avoid Codependent URRs

Agreement	My Responsibilities	Consequences for Breaking Agreements
I will not take on other people's problems in a RR.	To focus on my own issues and work to improve them.	Ruminating on problems that are not mine to fix.
I will not enter into a romantic relationship with someone who has more problems than I do.	Focus on how to deal with my own challenges.	Being so consumed with someone else's challenges that I ignore my own responsibilities.
I will not give advice to a problem-laden PRR about how they should deal with their challenging situations.	When asked for advice I will ask the person, "What do you think your options are?" and then be quiet.	Being drawn in by a PRR's neediness and becoming the sole source of his/her strength.
I will not try to rescue someone from the natural consequences of their bad decisions.	To leave a PRR who has more problems than I do.	Being in an unhappy romantic relationship that's consumed with problems, neediness, and helplessness. To try to control my RR's behavior or how he/she solves the problems.

How Can I Tell If I or My Partner Is Unhappy in Our Romantic Relationship?

We have reviewed what "seeds" an unhappy romantic relationship; now let's explore some of the things our partners do and some of the behaviors we exhibit when we are in an unhappy romantic relationship.

While there are entire books written about indications you are in an unhappy romantic relationship, here are several behaviors to look for.

Your Partner

- Doesn't spend much time at home.
- Spends less and less time with you.
- Prefers solitary rather than couple activities.
- Doesn't talk to you.
- Creates a wall of silence between you.
- Sparks arguments.
- Becomes increasingly critical of you and irritated with you.
- Has less patience with you.
- Communicates with you in a "snarky," disrespectful manner.
- Becomes distant.
- Appears uninterested in anything you have to say.

You

- Feel depressed about your home life.
- Hide your authentic self.
- Don't trust your partner and "investigate" his/her cell phone, emails, etc. to look for items that would validate your distrust.
- Don't want to make a commitment.
- Think that your life would be happier without your partner.
- Resent your partner.
- Engage in euphoric recall about past relationships.
- Spend less and less time together.
- Anger more easily.
- Find sex unsatisfying.
- Experience emotional distance.

If any of these items have manifested in your romantic relationship, chances are that you are in an unhappy romantic relationship! But if that is true, you already knew this. How long have you been unhappy? _____ years/months. How many more years/months are you willing to stay in your URR? _____ years/months.

Why We Stay in Unhappy Romantic Relationships—What Keeps Us Trapped

So many of us find ourselves cemented in an unhappy romantic relationship. We may want to leave, but something keeps us stuck. We may lack the finances that are necessary to move. It might be devastating to the children. The family would be upset. It's better to be with the devil we know than with the devil we don't know.

Often we can't even explain the reason(s) that keep us stuck. We just can't articulate it. Perhaps we can attribute this phenomenon to *unconscious fear*. Others of us are glued in the quicksand of *denial*. We tell ourselves it really isn't as bad as we think it is. We deny our unhappiness to ourselves and to others. We suffer in silence, or we make others suffer for our misery by blaming, nagging, yelling, and being overtly resentful. Then there are those of us who think we are *dependent* on our unhappy relationship, and reject any idea of changing lifestyles. We negate our own potential.

Let's have a look at some of the things that keep us trapped in our unhappy romantic relationships.

Why I Stay in Unhappy Romantic Relationships

Place a check by each of the reasons listed below that you believe have caused you to stay in an unhappy romantic relationship. If you need a review, turn to Chapter 3 and reread it.

☐ Mutual belongings
☐ Fear of the unknown
☐ Lack of autonomy
☐ Kids
☐ Regret about things you have done
☐ Hope for change
☐ Fear of dating
☐ Cost of divorce
☐ Concern about what others will think
☐ Hating to admit failure
☐ Inertia
☐ Fear of conflict
☐ Fear of change
☐ Fear of domestic violence

Add other reasons to the list.

☐ _____

☐ _____

☐ _____

☐ _____

☐ _____

The items that you have checked are the ones you need to overcome if you don't want to remain stuck in URRs. How do we do this? There is no simple answer. It requires courage to try something new. It requires patience to take baby steps toward becoming unstuck.

- Get more information about each of the items listed above that you have checked (books, articles, websites). You might want to start with *Codependent No More: How to Stop Controlling Others and Start Caring for Yourself* by Melody Beattie.
- Get counseling.
- Find a CoDA (Co-Dependents Anonymous) group in your community and go (it's free) and listen.
- Examine your family of origin teachings. Were you taught that unhappy relationships are "normal"? Did you grow up in a family that was ruled by drugs/alcohol, fear, silence, keeping secrets? Were you taught that there was something "wrong" with you? If you were, use the genogram template below to complete your own. The circles are females and the squares are males. The square or circle with the square or circle inside it identifies *you*. A genogram creates a picture of you and your family.

Next to each symbol in your genogram, write what that person told you when you were little. Also write about how they role modeled for you: for example, if your mother allowed herself to be hit and verbally abused, you were inadvertently taught that being in an abusive relationship is "normal"—not fun, but "normal." You were taught to fear conflict.

Compare what you were taught by your family of origin with the list of reasons (above) that you keep yourself in URRs. Do you find any similarities?

Here are a few interesting discoveries some of my patients made while creating their genogram:

"Every time my dad got mad, my mom would take me and my sister to the park. I hate it when people are mad."

"My dad told me that all his relatives would disown him if he divorced my mom."

"I was told that divorce costs too much; when I make a commitment I'd better stay in it no matter what."

"My brother was the favorite, so I have always believed I'm not lovable."

"My parents argued all the time and they threw things at each other. I learned that conflict brings physical harm."

"My mom always hoped my dad would stop drinking—he never did. I learned to hope that others will change."

What we learn in childhood often keeps us stuck in rules of the past that are not relevant in the present.

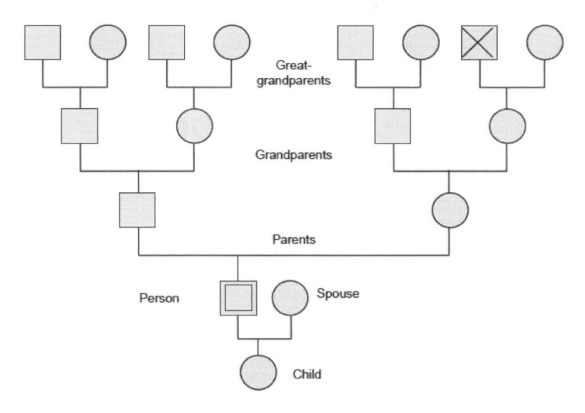

Mutual Belongings

So many of us in URRs say to ourselves that we don't want to leave our unhappiness because we have "so much stuff" together. Here is a list of "stuff." Rate it in the "Must Keep" and the "Can Let Go" columns. Add to the list at the end.

House:
☐ Must Keep
☐ Can Let Go
Children:
☐ Must Have Sole Custody
☐ Can Share Custody
Dog/Cat/Other Pets:
☐ Must Have Sole Custody
☐ Can Share Custody

Car:
☐ Must Keep
☐ Can Let Go

Television:
☐ Must Keep
☐ Can Let Go

Retirement Account:
☐ Must Keep All of It
☐ Will Have to Split It

Computer:
☐ Must Keep
☐ Can Let Go

Continue on with your list:

Item: _____
☐ Must Keep
☐ Can Let Go

Item: _____
☐ Must Keep
☐ Can Let Go

Item: _____
☐ Must Keep
☐ Can Let Go

Item: _____
☐ Must Keep
☐ Can Let Go

Must Keep
Total all the items you have identified as **"must keep."** Score _____

Can Let Go or Share
Total all the items you **"can let go"** or **"share."**
Score _____

Replaceable Items
How many of the "must keep" are replaceable?
Score _____

Deduct the "Replaceable" score from the "Must Keep" score.

These are the things that are keeping you *stuck* in your URR. These are the things that are in the way of *you* having a better life. Are they worth it?

Unconscious Fear

To understand "unconscious fear," we must have an elementary understanding of the brain, in particular the prefrontal cortex, the premotor cortex, and the amygdala. The amygdala is a major part of the brain's emotional center. It detours rational thought away from the area in our brain that is in charge of making good decisions (the prefrontal cortex). When the amygdala is "in charge," it inhibits our ability to make well-thought-out decisions. The amygdala also has an inhibiting effect on the premotor cortex, the area in the brain that stimulates us to get things done. Unconscious fear is the result of the amygdala's paralyzing effect on our rational thinking and our ability to move forward.

Furthermore, there is research that has discovered that our brains can register fear and we might not even know it. This phenomenon is due to what are called "mirroring" neurons. A mirroring neuron fires when you do an action and also when you simply watch someone else doing the same action. They allow us to determine other people's *intentions* as well as actions, and assist us in decoding facial expressions, whether we are observing a specific expression or making it ourselves. Therefore, when you and/or your romantic partner are unhappy, your "mirror neurons" enable you to immediately and instinctively understand each other's mood and intentions without saying a word.

What might be an example of this? Let's say your partner looks at you in disgust. You could automatically look back at your partner in the same way. Then, whatever meaning you have attached to the look of disgust will unconsciously signal you—usually to some degree of fear—unconscious fear. However, if your partner smiles at you, then, if you are like most, you will return the smile. If you have attached approval to the meaning of a smile, you will understand that as a form of acceptance.

To summarize, unconscious fear inhibits our rational thinking, reduces our ability to move forward, and can detect another person's moods and intentions. This is why many of us feel immobilized in unhappy romantic relationships. We feel powerless to do anything about it. We often can't put words to it. We can't identify our fear. We simply feel it. In some ways we intuit it. We remain stuck.

In our immobilization, our "stuckness," our unconscious fear, we then turn to those automatic reasons about why we can't change our situation. These are the fears that are commonly articulated:

- divorce
- disrupting the children
- being alone
- change
- inability to support oneself
- et cetera and ad nauseam—write your own list

Clark and Joann

I can't tell you how many of my patients have been stuck for years in their URR because of unexamined fear. Let's look at Clark and his wife, Joann, who report that they have "hated" each other for the past 15 years and don't know what to do.

CLARK: Thanks for seeing us, Doc. We are here because, well, to be frank, we hate each other and don't know what to do. We have two teenagers. We are afraid to change our life because of them.

THERAPIST: What do you mean when you say, "change our life"?

CLARK: Um, well, you know. Get a divorce or a separation?

THERAPIST: Joann, do you have the same feelings?

JOANN: Yes I do. I fell out of love with Clark years ago because he is so critical and emotionally abusive. Actually, I really don't like being around him, and I try to protect our two sons from his harshness and put-downs.

They frown at each other—mirror neurons in control.

THERAPIST: So are you both agreeing that this marriage is over and you want out?

Clark and Joann look at each other. There is silence for a moment. Clark frowns. Joann lowers her eyelids and won't look at her husband. Joann responds first.

JOANN: Yes! Definitely, yes!

CLARK: We've tried everything. I think it's time to call it a day.

THERAPIST: How long have you each felt this way?

They look at each other again as if one is waiting for the other to express a truth that has been long hidden.

CLARK: I'd say about 10 years.

JOANN: I'd say 15 years.

Clark looks at Joann in surprise.

THERAPIST: Are you considering divorce?

JOANN: Yes! But I'm afraid I can't make it on my own and that it will disrupt the kids.

THERAPIST: Have you met with a lawyer to discuss your options and your legal rights?

JOANN: No.

THERAPIST: Have you, Clark?

CLARK: Well, I've talked to some of my friends, but I haven't talked to a lawyer. But I'm not willing to throw away everything I have worked so hard to get—the cars, the house, the gym membership.

JOANN: You should have thought of that years ago when you wouldn't stop being mean all the time.

THERAPIST: Are you able to approach this as a business consultation and to put emotions and fears aside?

Note the amygdala has taken over.

JOANN: I'm not willing for me and the boys to live in poverty just because you want the house and the cars.

THERAPIST: I'm wondering. How might you find out what your rights are after a 25-year marriage? It seems that part of what is happening is that you are stuck in fear of the unknown. Is that right?

CLARK: What do you suggest, Doc?

THERAPIST: How do you think you can go about finding out what each of you is entitled to if you decide to separate or get a divorce?

This seems like a "no brainer," but Clark and Joann have been immobilized by their amygdalae, which have hijacked their ability to focus on solutions and to move forward from or make a decision about their long-term URR. In addition, their mirroring neurons have them "dancing" in disharmony with each other—one set of neurons following the other and vice versa.

JOANN: I just don't know what to do. I'm just so unhappy. I'm tired of being abused. I'm sick of being your whipping bag. There's nothing to do. I'm miserable.

Unconscious fear is returning Joann to being stuck—the same old dialogue she has been struggling with for the past 15 years.

CLARK: Whatever!

Notice that neither Clark or Joann focused on the question, "How do you think you can go about finding out what each of you are entitled to if you decide to separate or get a divorce?" They returned to their emotions and unconscious fear. Let's rework some of Clark and Joann's dialogue.

THERAPIST: How do you think you can go about finding out what each of you is entitled to if you decide to separate or get a divorce?

CLARK: Go to a lawyer and find out.

JOANN: Contact my friend, Arnie, who specializes in family law and make an appointment.

Here we have problem-solving, and unconscious fear is not driving the bus. Overcoming unconscious fear requires the willingness to take action. It requires the courage to think outside the box. It demands that we don't let our unexamined fears keep us stuck. Joann was trapped in bitterness and in the habit of blaming Clark for her URR. She had practiced self-righteous rage and being victimized by Clark for so long that in some ways it seemed "normal." It went on and on with no solution. Clark was stuck in his assigned (by Joann) role of being the perpetrator—the "mean" husband and father who victimized his wife and children.

Clark and Joann eventually overcame their unconscious fear because each went to an attorney to learn what the law says about a couple who have been married for 20 years, have two children, and share a wealth of community property. That is not to say the emotions about the marriage went away, but at least their emotions did not inhibit their respective desires to end the misery.

Unconscious fear requires us to make up a story about why we can't change anything in our URR. Joann's story was that she and her two sons would be impoverished. Clark's made-up story was that he would lose everything he had worked for. None of that happened—because of a little thing called family law. Clark and Joann's ignorance about their legal rights in a separation or divorce kept unconscious fears alive and well in their marriage. Their "stuck story" kept their un-researched fears in control.

Fear of divorce, fear of being alone, fear of change, and fear of an inability to support oneself are all based on stories we tell ourselves that are amygdala- (emotionally) driven. Rarely have I seen a patient who can articulate exactly what any of these fears actually mean to them. Let's return to Joann in a private therapy session:

> THERAPIST: Now that you have gotten legal advice, what are you considering as options to relieve some of your suffering?
> JOANN: Well, now I know that I won't be on the street and that my boys can continue on in the same school, I'm somewhat relieved. I just don't know what it will be like being alone.
> THERAPIST: What do you mean?
> JOANN: You know, being alone.
> THERAPIST: Could you explain that to me? I'm really not sure exactly what you mean.
> JOANN: I mean without a guy. You know, alone!
> THERAPIST: You mean without Clark?

Quiet edges its way into the room. Joann appears not to know what to say. To Joann, does being "alone" mean being without Clark? Does it mean abandoning her habit of blaming Clark for all that goes wrong? Does it mean leaving her unhappy daily interaction with her husband?

> JOANN: Hmm. I think it means without the familiarity of the last 20 years.
> THERAPIST: You mean without the unhappiness of the last 15 years?
> JOANN: I hate to say this, but my unhappiness has become familiar. (laughs) I don't even know what I am saying! What will I do without it?
> THERAPIST: Will you find new ways to be unhappy?

Will Joann seek those disapproving mirroring neurons that she has become accustomed to?

> JOANN: God! I hope not!

Joann is being held as an emotional hostage to fears she is unable to describe. They are emotions that aren't attached to words that explain them. Courageously, Joann continued in therapy until she was able to make her unconscious fears conscious. She became able to talk through the scary stories she had made up that weren't based on her present situation.

Unconscious fear can be wordless emotions hidden in our amygdala. These fears are immobilized by our premotor cortex and "frozen" there so we can't access them and search for a resolution. Unconscious fear is rationalized by made-up scary stories that we create for ourselves. These stories secure our complacency in our unhappiness. They manacle us from trying something we are not used to. They disallow us from risking change for something greater.

Fear of Change:
Your Status Quo Inventory

Status quo refers to the way things are in your relationship—the existing state of affairs.

What is the existing state of affairs in your unhappy romantic relationship? What are you afraid to change? Create your own inventory. Below are some ideas to get you started. Remember, this is *not* about how things used to be. This is about your *current* relationship. Check what applies to your URR.

1. Communication:
☐ Good
☐ Bad
☐ Mixed
Is it good enough that you do not want to change the communication dynamics with your partner?
☐ Yes
☐ No

2. Intimacy:
☐ Good
☐ Bad
☐ Mixed
Is it good enough that you do not want to change your partner's intimate behavior?
☐ Yes
☐ No

3. Respectful Treatment:
☐ Good
☐ Bad
☐ Mixed
Is it good enough that you do not want to change the way your partner treats you?
☐ Yes
☐ No

4. Fun Times Spent Together:

☐ Lots

☐ None

☐ Some

Is it good enough that you do not want to change how often you have fun together?

☐ Yes

☐ No

5. Expressions of Love:

☐ Yes

☐ No

☐ Sometimes

Are your partner's expressions of love good enough that you don't want to change them?

☐ Yes

☐ No

6. Enjoying Each Other's Company:

☐ Yes

☐ No

☐ Sometimes

☐ Rarely

Do you enjoy your partner's company enough that you do not want to change it?

☐ Yes

☐ No

7. Are you experiencing the "pursuit/panic" syndrome? Were you pursued heavily, got into a relationship, and now you are tenaciously holding on because your partner is withdrawing?

☐ Yes

☐ No

Is your "holding on" good enough that you do not want to change this dynamic?

☐ Yes

☐ No

8. Help with community responsibilities—such as loading the dishwasher, making the bed, etc.:
☐ Yes
☐ No
☐ Sometimes
Does your partner help with community responsibilities enough that you feel there is enough of a joint effort?
☐ Yes
☐ No

9. Are you happy with your home life?:
☐ Yes
☐ No
☐ Sometimes
Are you happy enough with your home life that you don't want to change it?
☐ Yes
☐ No

10. Are you happy with the manner in which your partner treats the children?
☐ Yes
☐ No
☐ Sometimes
Are you happy enough with the way your partner treats the children that you don't want to change it?
☐ Yes
☐ No

Add your own items to this list. A template is provided on the next page. Add up the items with "Yes" responses. Add up items with "No" responses. Add up items with "Sometimes" or "Mixed" responses. Compare your responses. All the items in the "No" column are the ones that you are afraid to change!

Template for "Fear of Change" Worksheet

Are you happy with your _____?

☐ Yes

☐ No

☐ Sometimes

Are you happy enough with _____ that you don't want to change it?

Are you happy with your _____?

☐ Yes

☐ No

☐ Sometimes

Are you happy enough with _____ that you don't want to change it?

Are you happy with your _____?

☐ Yes

☐ No

☐ Sometimes

Are you happy enough with _____ that you don't want to change it?

Cognitive Distortions

What are cognitive distortions (CDs)?[21] They are two fancy words used to describe a list of common inaccurate ways of thinking that we use to reinforce negative thoughts or emotions. Cognitive distortions help us tell ourselves things that sound rational or accurate but actually serve to keep our suffering in our URRs in place. Sometimes our thoughts automatically go to well-rehearsed and practiced cognitive distortions so that we see no alternative ways to consider problem-solving. Cognitive distortions are the underlying structure for the made-up stories we tell ourselves that assist in keeping us from leaving unhappy romantic relationships.

For the purposes of this book, the list of CDs provided below addresses the ones that are most often used to deny the truth and/or our feelings in our unhappy romantic relationships. Within each type of CD listed are examples of the stories we tell ourselves that keep our negative thinking in place and that keep us stuck. Additionally, there are examples of alternative ways of thinking that will help lead us out of our made-up stories and out of the cognitive distortion that provides the glue for our "stuckness."

---

[21] *See articles by John M. Grohol in References.*

Denial

What is denial? It is *not* a river in Egypt, as the old joke goes. Denial is believing that something is not true when it is. Denial is packed with minimization, rationalization, and excuses that provide the adhesive that keep us stuck in unhappy romantic relationships. Denial is accompanied by the belief that things will change, and the good times will return despite evidence to the contrary. Beliefs based on denial are founded on air and *not* on changes that our partner has made to alter behaviors that are unacceptable to us and that violate our values. Many of us in URRs practice denial by telling ourselves that the possibility of a better life is impossible. This belief is based on a fantasy forecast of the future—*a made-up story*!

Denial

"My boyfriend is smoking a lot of pot, but it is just temporary, and I know it's because he can't stand stress."

Versus Breaking Through the Distortion

"My boyfriend's pot smoking irritates me and violates my value about having a partner whose mind is not chemically altered. I see no evidence that he is going to quit."

Denial

"I know that my partner doesn't really mean the terrible things he says to me. If I keep explaining how much this wounds me, I know one day he/she will understand and stop being so abusive."

Versus Breaking Through the Distortion

"My partner and I have been together for two years, and for much of that time he/she has been demeaning and insulting when I don't agree with something. I don't see any behaviors that suggest that he/she is working toward a change."

Catastrophizing

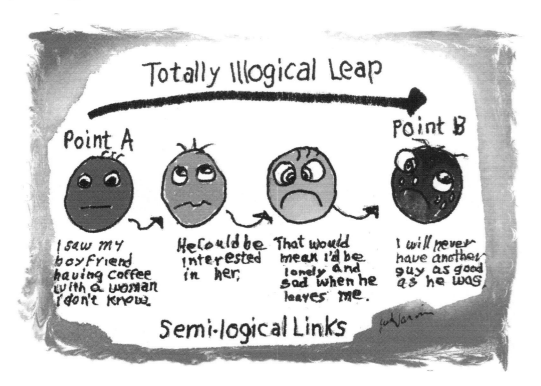

Catastrophizing is a way we minimize or magnify events and behaviors based on distortions and made-up stories. Catastrophizing is usually accompanied by the "what if?" mind game one plays with oneself. In catastrophizing we expect disaster to strike no matter what. These expectations of harm, failure, and tragedy glue us to our URR because our URR provides us with the illusion of safety and security—no matter what price we may pay.

Catastrophizing

"I will never be able to make it on my own if I leave my partner. I'll be destitute. My kids and I will starve!"

Versus Breaking Through the Distortion

"My kids and I have never starved. I will find a job so I can give them a better life than the one we are living right now. I will also look at government assistance options."

Catastrophizing

"What if I never find another partner? No one would ever want me."

Versus Breaking Through the Distortion

"Whether or not I find another partner, I will be fine."

Personalization

In URRs, personalization can manifest as seeing oneself as the cause of your partner's dissatisfaction. We think we are the cause of every mistake or mood. To support this type of thinking, our partner often tells us that indeed, everything *is* our fault!

Personalization

"If I hadn't overcooked lunch, my partner would have had a better time watching football. Now he/she's upset—and it's all my fault."

Versus Breaking Through the Distortion

"I overcooked lunch. I wasn't paying attention. My partner looks upset. I'm going to play tennis."

Personalization

"I was stuck in traffic, and that made me late to pick up my wife. Even though I called, she looks so upset. It's all my fault."

Versus Breaking Through the Distortion

"Horrible traffic made me late to pick up my wife. Now she looks upset. Traffic seems to be getting worse lately."

Control Fallacies

External and internal fallacies are two types of faulty reasoning that can lead to despair and suffering in our romantic relationships. They provide us with ways to make unsound arguments that can keep us stuck in URRs. They assist us in eroding our self-esteem.

External Control

If we believe we are controlled by other people or by outside forces we will see ourselves as a victim of fate. No matter what we do, we are powerless over the outcome of events.

External Control Fallacy

"I just can't seem to find a good partner. With my luck, I know I will never find one."

Versus Breaking Through the Distortion

"I think I will take a break from romantic relationships and explore the reasons I keep making such poor choices."

External Control Fallacy

"Maybe it's my fate to be alone. I'm just not made for having a happy relationship."

Versus Breaking Through the Distortion

"I select people who don't hold the same values I have. This is a cause of my URRs. I need to figure out a better way of selecting potential romantic relationships."

Internal Control

Assuming responsibility for the pain and happiness of everyone around us—especially our partner. Even when there is no indication that anyone is upset, folks with internal control cognitive distortions often ask, "Is there something wrong?" This question provides a way of scanning one's environment for discontent—which of course, is "your fault."

Internal Control Fallacy

"I see you aren't eating your dinner. Is it because of something I did?"

Versus Breaking Through the Distortion

"I suspect you aren't eating your dinner. If you're done, I'll clear the table."

Internal Control Fallacy

QUESTION: Is there something wrong?
ANSWER: No
THOUGHT: He/she looks unhappy; I wonder what I did?!

Versus Breaking Through the Distortion

QUESTION: Is there something wrong? You are looking tired and sad.
ANSWER: No
THOUGHT: I'd better call Betty about our bowling date tomorrow.

Blaming

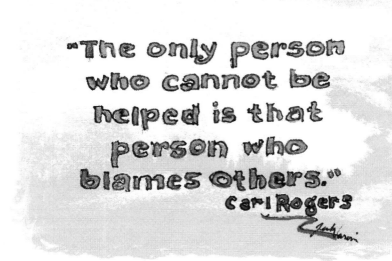

"The only person who cannot be helped is that person who blames others."
Carl Rogers

With blaming, we hold ourselves responsible for every problem—we blame ourselves for how our partner treats us, for how he/she talks to us. Additionally, we often are the recipient of our partner's blame. We struggle with the accusations that are often not accurate.

Blaming

"If I just hadn't brought up that topic then my partner wouldn't have had a fit and started throwing things."

Versus Breaking Through the Distortion

"My partner has an anger problem and acts out in inappropriate ways."

Blaming

"My spouse says I talk to my girlfriend too much and that is why he's in such a foul mood when he comes home from work. He says I spend half the day on the phone—which is not true—and that's why the house is a mess."

Versus Breaking Through the Distortion

"While the house is not perfect, it's not a mess, considering we have two small children. I do talk to my girlfriend every day for at least 30 minutes. I am an adult. I can manage my time. I am not taking responsibility for his moods."

"Should," "Must," and "Ought"

We fight a constant internal battle about what we "should," "shouldn't," "ought," or "must" do. These "shoulds," "musts," and "oughts" provide the baseline for how we guilt ourselves into the need to be perfect. Because we aren't perfect (and I have yet to meet a perfect person—let me know if you find one), we keep trying harder and harder. We hold ourselves to an impossible standard, and remain stuck in our URR with the idea that if only we were "better," our partner would be more considerate, loving, etc. We feel guilty about our lack of imperfection! "Should," "must," and "ought" are words that make us automatically wrong. Replacing these words with "could," "may," and "might" imply choice. They are much less judgmental.

Shoulds

"I should have done a better job ironing Tom's shirts. He was upset the crease was crooked and the back still had wrinkles. It's all my fault. After all, I offered to do the ironing."

Versus Breaking Through the Distortion

"I could have done a better ironing job if I had more practice. I don't like ironing. Tom could do this himself. I'm not going to offer any more."

Musts

"I must make more of an effort to be happy so Betsy will be happy too."

Versus Breaking Through the Distortion

"As long as I'm kind, thoughtful, and respectful, Betsy's happiness is up to her. I might compliment her more often."

Oughts

"I ought to be friendlier to my boyfriend's friend, even though he insulted me."

Versus Breaking Through the Distortion

"I could make an effort to be friendlier to my boyfriend's friend even though he insulted me. On the other hand, I might decide to do something else when his friend is around."

Emotional Reasoning

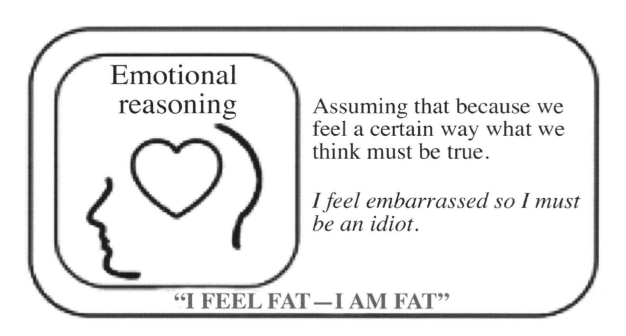

We believe that what we intuit or feel is automatically true. We tell ourselves, "I feel it, so it must be true." We disregard facts and observed evidence, and conclude our emotional response proves something is true.

Emotional Reasoning

"I feel that if I had a college degree my partner would treat me better."

Versus Breaking Through the Distortion

"My partner's ex had a college degree and he treated her terribly. There is evidence that he is abusive to women."

If you "feel" inferior then you believe you are. You assume that your (often unhealthy) emotions reflect the way things really are. We stay in our URR because we "feel" that if we got more education the relationship would be happy.

Emotional Reasoning

"I feel that my girlfriend is cheating. I saw her at a coffeeshop with a guy."

Versus Breaking Through the Distortion

"I feel that my girlfriend is cheating but there is no evidence that this is true. We are together all the time, and she has lots of friends."

Fallacy of Change

With our partner: We expect our partner to change to suit us. We believe that if we lecture, reason, and explain to him/her enough, he/she will change and then we will be happy—because our hopes for happiness depend entirely on him/her changing. We get stuck in our URR believing that all the relationship problems will be solved if our spouse/boyfriend/girlfriend would only change! Getting our loved one to change often becomes our "mission," and serves to diminish what happiness there may have been.

Fallacy of Change

"If my spouse would only talk to me with respect, then we would have a happier relationship. I've told him/her over and over that every time I'm called a bad name I feel awful. Nothing changes."

Versus Breaking Through the Distortion

"For the past three years I have been called names in spite of requests for change. Evidence supports the idea that my spouse isn't going to change. I need to decide if I am going to stay in an abusive relationship."

With ourselves: We stay stuck in the belief that if only we could change that would lead our partner to change as well. We often struggle with making changes in order to please our partner. Demeaning ourselves about our own challenges in making changes puts responsibility squarely at our feet.

Fallacy of Change

"I am going to stop drinking, and then maybe my spouse will stop drinking too."

Versus Breaking through the Distortion

"My spouse doesn't want to stop drinking, and I believe him."

Heaven's Reward Fallacy

With this cognitive distortion, our belief is that if we sacrifice and deny ourselves happiness we will get a payoff. We often feel angry when the reward never materializes.

"Heaven's Reward" Fallacy

"If I suffer through this relationship by staying and supporting my girlfriend, I know I'll probably get some kind of reward."

We often conceptualize the reward as other people's admiration of our sacrifice, or going to heaven as a reward for being good. Much of this is based on our fear of how others and God might perceive us.

Versus Breaking Through the Distortion

"Suffering and sacrificing don't come with rewards."

Magnification and Minimization

Magnification and minimization are the tendency to magnify the positive attributes of someone else while minimizing your own.

Magnification and Minimization

"My girlfriend is so smart! She has a college degree and is a manager. My education and job aren't nearly as good as hers."

Versus Breaking Through the Distortion

"My girlfriend is so smart! She has a college degree and is a manager. I'm glad I have talents in other areas. It makes our relationship so much more interesting."

Jumping to Conclusions

When we jump to conclusions we are assuming that we know what others are thinking or feeling. We also assume we know why they act the way they do. We believe we can determine how others feel about us. We make up stories about what others think and feel and these stories are usually negative. They are stories that lead to suffering.

Jumping to Conclusions

"I know Greg is thinking how ugly I look tonight. I wish he thought I was really attractive, but I bet he actually hates how I look!"

Versus Breaking Through the Distortion

"Greg, how do I look tonight?"

As said above, the cognitive distortions described here are the ones that usually provide the glue that keeps us in our unhappy romantic relationships. We must free ourselves. If we are going to find happiness in our romantic relationships, the thinking that has kept us stuck in our URRs has to change. Work to undo your cognitive distortions. Use the examples provided above as a way to break through them.

Other Issues That Keep
Us Stuck in Our URRs

There are uncountable reasons why people avoid leaving URRs. Listed below are some of the reasons that patients have provided over the years. How do we work through these fears?

Mutual Belongings

"We just bought a house/TV/car together."

Are you allowing material items to keep you stuck and unhappy? What about the dog or cat? The idea of leaving some of our "stuff" with the person we are leaving is often driven by irrational animosity. By focusing on material losses our suffering only increases. By focusing on the loss of a loved pet we anguish in sadness. To avoid this pain, we often stay in our URR and direct our affection from our partner to our pet, or our house, car, etc. We stay because it is easier than foraging through to the unknown.

Fear of the Unknown

Fear of the unknown is that wordless feeling that we call anxiety. We often say to ourselves, *I don't know what will happen if I leave my URR*! Of course you don't know. In fact, you didn't know what would happen when you got involved with your then-romantic relationship. If you are like others, you might have made up a story about how wonderful the relationship would be, and now you find yourself unhappy and afraid. If we spent as much time examining our fears about getting into a romantic relationship as we do about getting out of our now-URR, many of us wouldn't enter into RRs as quickly as we do! Remember the "love cocktail" and limerence? They put our blinders on and assist us in discounting fears. See "My Fears About Dating" in Chapter 3.

Lack of Autonomy

You've given your independence away and have practiced looking to your partner to organize your life, manage bills, make major decisions, decide where to eat dinner, what vacation to take, etc. What happened to *you*? Where did *you* go? The challenge of becoming independent and giving up the "gift" of abdicating responsibility for decision-making can keep our feet stuck in our URR.

Kids

This is a huge reason for staying in a URR. However, unhappiness has a tendency to permeate one's home. Unhappiness in the home affects children in a very negative way. Whether to stay in a URR because of the children is a decision one must make. With having to make such a decision, it is critical to protect all children from physical, sexual, and emotional abuse. Is that going on in your URR? Are you violating your values by staying? Check yourself to rule out the "Heaven's Reward Fallacy" cognitive distortion: "I'll suffer now because I'll find happiness in the afterlife." Once the decision is made, you don't get to act out because you are miserable. Whatever you have decided—to stay or to leave— *you* made the choice so *you* get to role model for your children how to get through difficult times. This is not to say that you can't change your decision, but while you're abiding by your current decision, make the most of it.

Regret

Because we have remorse about and feel responsible for events in the past that have caused unhappiness in our URR, we try to make up for our errors. We live in regret. Unless one has healthy emotional attachment to the person we have wronged, staying in a URR because we are sorry will keep us stuck in the past. Because our actions have caused others disappointment, despair, or distress is not *the* reason to stay in a URR. While we certainly need to make amends to anyone we have inadvertently distressed, lingering so we can keep whipping ourselves only leads to further suffering.

There is another element to regret. It is realizing that at age 40, for example, you've invested a long time in being with the wrong person.

Hope

The lure that someone will change if we *hope* enough is a practice that rarely brings happiness. All hope is is a statement that we are not happy in the present, so we hope for change. In URRs, that hope is usually aimed at our partner—"I hope Susie will stop drinking"; "I hope John will get a job." Hope is the desire for something to be different. Hope is an indication that the present is unsatisfactory.

Fear of Dating

Many of us who feel stuck in URRs find ourselves practicing negative self-talk that serves to keep us frozen. We often ask ourselves, *Who else would want me?* Fear of dating is often tied to fear of rejection and fear that all the awful things we say to ourselves will be verified by a date—verified by a stranger who doesn't know us and whom we don't know.

Dating is about having fun. Is that what it's about for you? List your fears about dating. Where did they come from? Who in your family of origin taught you to hold yourself in such low esteem? In addition, consider that it might be really beneficial to be on your own for a while. See "My Fears About Dating" in Chapter 3.

Divorce Is Too Expensive

There are many ways that one can separate from a URR without spending gazillions of dollars on attorney fees. So many people think they are stuck in their URR because of money, but they have not investigated their options. See "Cost of Divorce" in Chapter 5.

Religious Beliefs

Many religions disallow separation or divorce. What does your partner's religion teach about this? What does your religion teach about this? What are your values around staying in a URR *no matter what*? If you don't do this research *before* you enter into a committed romantic relationship, you might find yourself stuck. If this is the case, explore what your options are.

Concern About What Family/Friends Will Think

If you are in a URR and you are staying due to concern about what others will think, what you are actually saying is that *you* fear you have a family and/or friends who don't care much about you as an individual, that they care more about your partnership than they do about your individual happiness.

Hating to Admit Failure

Translation: "success" for me means staying in an unhappy romantic relationship.

Inertia

When we are apathetic about our URR there is no motivation to change things, so we remain right where we are—stuck. We become accustomed to our unhappiness. To overcome inertia requires work, as opposed to just making do and settling. Familiar doesn't necessarily mean good.

Fear of Change

We could actually relate this back to "Fear of the Unknown." Fear of change involves choosing your URR over the possibility of happiness because we have learned to be somewhat comfortable in the familiarity of our unhappiness. For those of us who are paralyzed by this fear, please examine exactly what the status quo in your URR actually is.

Hidden Reasons for Staying in Your URR

Are you getting "secret payoffs" from staying in your URR? Some people have been taught that being a caretaker and/or trying to rescue/fix someone is the role one should take in a romantic relationship. They have been taught (usually by members of their family of origin) that rescuing, saving a RR is the way to being thought of as a "good" person. Introduce yourself to books about codependency, and examine what it would be like to be free of projects to fix.

Practicalities of Everyday Life

After being in a relationship for a while, there seems to be a division of responsibility. In our unhappiness with the relationship, we often become quite comfortable with splitting the rent, being on our partner's health insurance, etc. It can be scary to envision taking on all the responsibilities that have been shared. See "Fear of Change: Your Status Quo Inventory" in Chapter 3 for some suggestions about how to sort the "practicalities" out.

After reading this chapter, we hopefully understand some of the reasons we feel stuck in our URR. Our unconscious fears, cognitive distortions, family of origin issues, and an array of other thoughts and beliefs keeps us stuck. So now what? First we need to decide whether to stay or leave our URR. The next chapter will assist you with decision-making, and provide you with ways to stay and ways to leave if that is what you decide to do.

Fear of Conflict

Just what does this mean to you? What is your history with conflict? For most of us, conflict is not about negotiating it is about "winning." When invested in winning, emotions (the amygdala) can take over and problem-solving goes out the window. If we can redirect our fear of conflict to a search for meeting challenges calmly by seeking a solution, then some of our fears might be put to rest. However, if we are involved in a URR in which our partner is violent when going for the "win" in an argument, put *your* safety first. Set limits for what is OK and what is *not* OK during a disagreement.

What Is Your History of Conflict?

How do you define conflict? Many of us are afraid of conflict, but we haven't defined what "conflict" means to us. Check those that apply or describe in your own words your definition of conflict.

- ☐ A fight to the end
- ☐ A serious disagreement or argument
- ☐ A quarrel
- ☐ A dispute
- ☐ An antagonistic state or action
- ☐ Divergent ideas or interests
- ☐ An active disagreement between people with opposing opinions or principles

Write your own definitions:

_____

_____

_____

_____

_____

What is your history with conflict? What are your beliefs about conflict that keep you avoiding problem-solving? Check those that apply or write in your own history or beliefs about conflict.

☐ People leave me if I disagree with them.
☐ I will fall victim to aggression by the opposing person.
☐ I will be embarrassed.
☐ Trying to explain myself is exhausting.
☐ Conflict was/is not allowed in my family of origin.
☐ I grew up in a household in which conflict resulted in screaming and yelling, physical, emotional, or sexual abuse, so it was safer to stay miserable and not say anything.
☐ If I disagree I won't be liked.
☐ I was shamed if I disagreed.
☐ I suffer retaliation from people I disagree with.
☐ When I express an opinion I'm proven wrong.
☐ In a conflict I get so angry I can't express myself.
☐ Every time I express a different opinion, I hurt someone's feelings.
☐ I was taught to defer to other people's opinions.
☐ I have a history of being in critical relationships, so I freeze up when I sense an upcoming conflict. I become afraid.
☐ After a conflict I have difficulty feeling an attachment for another person. My family members used anger to break connections.
☐ I never win, so I might as well be quiet.
☐ It's not worth the energy because nothing ever changes.

Write your own history with conflict:

_____
_____
_____
_____
_____

The items you have checked form the foundation for your fear of conflict. They are the reasons you don't stand up for your own values. Have you brought your fears from the past into your current relationship? Are you afraid to express yourself in your current relationship? Does this cause you suffering? Identifying for yourself that you are in a URR can be very scary because if we decide to "save" ourselves, conflict will usually accompany that decision. Remember, fear of conflict keeps you trapped in it forever!

My Fears About Dating

We must decide if we are dating to find a mate or if we are dating to just have fun. Remember limerence? Remember the "love cocktail"? These will pull you into "love" with a stranger. "Just having fun" may lead to friendship and eventually a long-lasting *happy* (what a concept) romantic relationship!

What are your fears about dating? Let's look at some of the common fears many of my patients have shared with me and see if any of them resonate with you:

No one will want me:

☐ Yes

☐ No

I'm too old:

☐ Yes

☐ No

I'm too fat:

☐ Yes

☐ No

I have too many wrinkles:

☐ Yes

☐ No

I have cellulite:

☐ Yes

☐ No

I have scars:

☐ Yes

☐ No

My feet are so ugly:

☐ Yes

☐ No

My glasses are so thick:

☐ Yes

☐ No

I look so ugly in the morning:

☐ Yes

☐ No

I have thinning hair:

☐ Yes

☐ No

I have "Popeye" arms:

☐ Yes

☐ No

I'm balding:

☐ Yes

☐ No

I have erectile dysfunction:

☐ Yes

☐ No

I have an STD and it is so embarrassing to tell anyone:

☐ Yes

☐ No

Now add to this list in the space below. What are your fears about dating?

Do you see how many of these reasons for fearing dating have to do with intimacy? Do you really think that with casual dating you need to discuss your cellulite or erectile dysfunction? Again, look at this list—they are all negative, unkind, harsh thoughts. They are judgments about yourself on a very personal level. Do you think these thoughts before meeting up with your girl or guy friends? Do you think them before attending a sporting event? Probably not.

Let's try to change our thinking around:

- My date and I are going to the zoo. That will be such fun.
- I've been looking forward to seeing this movie and I'm so glad I have a date who invited me.
- I was invited for coffee. I am looking forward to meeting a new person and to a latte.
- I love having conversations with _____. He/she is so interesting.

Do you see how this type of thinking centers around activities? Give yourself a vacation from all the negativity that you create around the idea of dating. Have fun and let go of the outcome!

One more word: I have many patients who comb Match.com and eHarmony and PlentyOfFish. Here is an accumulation of their experiences:

- "Everyone puts pictures on the site that were taken 20 years ago."
- "The people I have met on dating sites just want sex."
- "Are all the unemployed people on dating sites?"
- "I was scammed and sent $5,000 to a guy in Iran so he could fly home—his credit card was stolen. I am so upset because I thought we had a good relationship."
- "I met a woman who said she was divorced for three years, and it turned out she was still married!"
- "This guy told me he had no kids, and he turned out to have four."
- "I went to lunch, and the entire time this guy showed me pictures of different kinds of trout he had caught."
- "I was communicating on one of these sites with someone who only wanted to talk about sex."

There are many folks out there who are not a dating or a romantic match for *you*. Not every dating experience will be fun. It will, however, be an adventure. Those who enter the dating scene with the idea of immediately finding a romantic match will be very disappointed and thus, their fears about dating will be actualized. As a final note—*develop a sense of humor!*

CHAPTER 4

Should I Stay?
How Do I Leave?

Should I Stay in My URR?

Only you can decide if you need to stay in your URR. Answer these questions:

1. Am I suffering in this URR?
☐ Yes
☐ No

2. Can I afford a room, apartment, or other living arrangement? Can I move in with a relative?
☐ Yes
☐ No

3. Would I be willing to experiment with a trial separation?
☐ Yes
☐ No

4. Would leaving be better or worse for the children *in the long run*?
☐ Better
☐ Worse

When answering this question, remember we are looking at the long-term good. Kids have a way of picking up their caregiver's emotions and taking them in. If the adults are depressed or anxious in their URR, chances are the children will be depressed or anxious also.

5. Is the feeling gone in my relationship?
☐ Yes
☐ No
Can I get it back?
☐ Yes
☐ No

6. Has there been an unforgivable betrayal in my romantic relationship like infidelity, deception, or abuse?
☐ Yes
☐ No

7. Has my partner become dismissive or neglectful?
☐ Yes
☐ No

8. Does my partner criticize me most of the time?
☐ Yes
☐ No

9. Am I emotionally responsive with my partner?
☐ Yes
☐ No

10. Am I emotionally disengaged?
☐ Yes
☐ No

11. Our sex life is unsatisfactory.
☐ Yes
☐ No

12. I have lost respect for my partner.
☐ Yes
☐ No

13. Our relationship consists of arguing all the time or having no communication at all.
☐ Yes
☐ No

14. I am so tired of trying to engage in this relationship I can't force myself to try to mend it one more time.
☐ Yes
☐ No

15. I am no longer interested in meeting my partner's needs.
☐ Yes
☐ No

16. My partner and I live separate lives and I don't care what he/she is doing.
☐ Yes
☐ No

17. We talk about trivia rather than substantial topics.
☐ Yes
☐ No

18. I and my partner are just parents—that is the extent of our relationship.
☐ Yes
☐ No

19. I love the dog/cat more than my partner.
☐ Yes
☐ No

20. My partner and I have different goals for the future.
☐ Yes
☐ No

21. Is there contempt in your URR?
☐ Yes
☐ No

Look over the worksheet above. The questions address most of the components that make a good relationship—trust, attention, support, emotional engagement, a healthy sex life, respect and caring for one's partner, problem-solving, communication, having common goals, intimacy. If you have tried to work on your relationship and those efforts have failed, you can choose to live in the vacancy of the current relationship, or you can consider leaving. These are hard decisions. If there is nothing left in the relationship, make a list of the reasons you are staying and review the previous chapter for further clarity. Living in your fears does not provide happiness. Remember, for every relationship you hold on to there is another one that may be missed.

Ways I Have Tried to Save My Relationship

Leaving a relationship is a huge decision. Before we consider leaving, let's take a look at ways many of my patients have worked on turning their relationship around for the better.

Kate and Shelly

Kate and Shelly met at a gay rights rally and found that they shared political passions. Much of their relationship revolved around lobbying and protesting. They dated for six months, moved in together for six months, and then got married.

Their first argument centered on Shelly wanting to hang out with a group of friends who Kate didn't like. Kate's complaint was that they rarely had private time together, and when there was an opportunity, Shelly usually opted to hang out with her pals.

What Kate tried:

1. Talking with Shelly about how much she wanted to spend time with her to "have fun."

Result: Shelly promised to do better.

Nothing changed.

2. Sharing with Shelly how hurt her feelings were when Shelly had promised to do better, but continued to hang with her pals at every opportunity.

Result: Shelly told Kate that she worked hard and that being with her friends allowed her to de-stress. She also told Kate that she was tired of being nagged.

Nothing changed.

3. Kate made an effort to ignore her emotions and stop talking about the issue.

Nothing changed.

4. Kate asked Shelly if she could go with her to hang out with her pals. Shelly hesitantly agreed. Kate went. Kate still didn't like Shelly's friends.

Nothing changed.

5. Kate became angry and told Shelly she didn't feel like she had a partner. Shelly became angry and told Kate, "If you don't like it, too bad. I feel suffocated when you try to guilt me into staying home. What's there to do? Watch TV?"

Nothing changed.

6. Kate suggested that she and Shelly go to couple's counseling. Shelly hesitantly agreed. They attended three sessions. After each session, Kate and Shelly had huge arguments about what was said during the therapy.

Nothing changed.

7. Kate told Shelly she felt that she was avoiding her during rallies. Kate pointed out that they used to march together but now, Shelly was protesting with the group of pals whom Kate didn't like. Kate told Shelly she was feeling very alone in their relationship.

Result: Shelly told Kate that she felt suffocated.

Nothing changed.

Walt and Claudia

Walt and Claudia met online. They dated six months before Walt asked Claudia to marry him. They married a year later. Their courtship was done via dinner dates, movies, hiking, and bowling—lots of "away from home" activities. Walt was often at Claudia's house, but Claudia was rarely at Walt's. The couple married six months after Walt's proposal. This was a second marriage for both. Walt had a 15-year-old son, Barry, who was having problems in school, and Claudia had two daughters, Penny and Marsha, who attended the same high school as Walt's son. The girls were class officers and cheerleaders at their high school.

Walt and Claudia sold their respective homes and bought a home together so each of their children would have their own room. They felt their newly blended family needed more space "so everyone would be happy." Claudia knew that Barry had a history of drinking and using drugs. She convinced herself that with the "good influence of my daughters" and with a beautiful new bedroom, Walt's son would see the error of his ways.

The couple joined together to create "home rules." One of the rules was that no one under the age of 21 could use drugs or drink alcohol in their home. They discussed this with their teens. Barry said, "Whatever." Penny and Marsha said, "We don't do that anyway."

As the moving van made its final delivery to their new home, Claudia was carrying some items upstairs and noticed an aroma "that smelled like manure." She walked into Barry's room, and there he was on the bed, smoking a joint. Claudia told him, "There is none of that allowed in our home. Put that out. I'm going to get your father." Walt lectured Barry and grounded him for a week.

Claudia became hyper-vigilant. She began to check on Barry's every move and report it to Walt. Barry hated Claudia for the monitoring.

After that event, things appeared to calm down in the house. Barry, Penny, and Marsha seemed to get along, although Barry mainly kept to himself.

A month after taking up residency in their new home, Claudia again detected "that manure smell." Suspecting where it was coming from, and without knocking, Claudia opened Barry's door, and there he was sitting at his desk smoking something out of "some kind of apparatus." Claudia later learned that Barry owned a hookah.

While standing in Barry's room, Claudia called Walt at work. She reported what she had discovered. Barry got up and left the room. Then he left the house. He did not return for two days.

When Walt arrived home from work, Claudia told him "this cannot continue!" She wanted to know how long Barry had been smoking marijuana and drinking. She wanted to know how Walt had dealt with this when it first became a problem. Claudia told Walt that he had to "fix" this problem. Walt said he would.

Nothing changed.

Being a resourceful woman, Claudia began researching about addiction. She attended Al-Anon "as a visitor." Claudia was determined to solve Barry's problem because it was "ruining our happy home." Claudia invited Walt to attend Al-Anon with her. Walt said there was a sporting event he had to watch. Claudia went to the meeting with Penny and Marsha.

Nothing changed.

Three more times Claudia caught Barry either drinking or smoking pot in his room. The ritual became that Claudia would call Walt at work, Walt would come home and ground and lecture Barry, Claudia and her daughters would go to Al-Anon.

Result: Claudia and Walt's relationship became contentious. Claudia told Walt he "had to deal with your son's problem." Walt told Claudia he was trying, but "my efforts just aren't good enough for you."

Nothing changed.

Claudia begged Walt to attend an Al-Anon meeting she had found that was comprised of parents struggling with teens who had substance abuse problems. Walt told her he was busy and commented, "You know, this is just a stage, all kids do it. You are making too much out of this!"

Something changed: Claudia got angrier and more protective of her daughters. There were new relationship dynamics:

- Claudia was furious and verbally attacked Walt on a regular basis.
- Penny and Marsha spent more time in their rooms.
- Walt became defensive and stayed later and later at the office.
- The foundation for a wall of silence had been laid.
- Walt continued to say that there was no real problem because "every kid experiments."
- Claudia was on a mission to have Walt read about addiction. Walt was "busy."

In this scenario, we have a "problem-solver" in a relationship with a "procrastinator." They are involved with a serious issue—teen substance abuse. Being the stepmother without power, Claudia is powerless.

In the end there was a change. Claudia, Penny, and Marsha left and moved to an apartment. They reported that they were much happier.

So here you have it. Two scenarios in which one person tried to improve the relationship by offering suggestions about how to make those changes while the other person resisted.

How have *you* tried to be heard, collaborate, offer ideas for change, or make efforts to improve yourself when your partner refuses to join you?

Take this inventory and add others at the end of it.

List of Ways I Have Tried to Save My URR

1. Had a discussion:
☐ Yes
☐ No
Did it help change the situation?
☐ Yes
☐ No

2. Had a second discussion:
☐ Yes
☐ No
Did it help change the situation?
☐ Yes
☐ No

3. Nagged:
☐ Yes
☐ No
Did it help change the situation?
☐ Yes
☐ No

4. Begged:
☐ Yes
☐ No
Did it help change the situation?
☐ Yes
☐ No

5. Yelled:
☐ Yes
☐ No
Did it help change the situation?
☐ Yes
☐ No

6. Went to counseling:

☐ Yes

☐ No

Did it help change the situation?

☐ Yes

☐ No

7. Tried to make my partner jealous:

☐ Yes

☐ No

Did it help change the situation?

☐ Yes

☐ No

8. Read books on the subject:

☐ Yes

☐ No

Did it help change the situation?

☐ Yes

☐ No

9. Tried to have more sex or be sexier for my partner:

☐ Yes

☐ No

Did it help change the situation?

☐ Yes

☐ No

10. Tried to ignore my own needs:

☐ Yes

☐ No

Did it help change the situation?

☐ Yes

☐ No

11. Written your partner a letter addressing the issue and saying what you need changed:

☐ Yes

☐ No

Did it help change the situation?

☐ Yes

☐ No

12. Took a vacation with my partner:
☐ Yes
☐ No
Did it help change the situation?
☐ Yes
☐ No

13. Created date nights:
☐ Yes
☐ No
Did it help change the situation?
☐ Yes
☐ No

14. Took a vacation by yourself for alone time:
☐ Yes
☐ No
Did it help change the situation?
☐ Yes
☐ No

Now add on to this list noting other things you have tried, and whether they helped change the situation.

Other things tried	Did it help change the situation?
	☐ Yes ☐ No
	☐ Yes ☐ No
	☐ Yes ☐ No
	☐ Yes ☐ No
	☐ Yes ☐ No
	☐ Yes ☐ No

Total the Yeses: _____

The "yeses" indicate the number of things you have tried to save your URR.

Total the Nos: _____

The "nos" are the number of times your attempts were not met with success.

Look at all the things you have tried. If you have had some successes in creating change within your relationship, do more of what you did. If you have had few or no successes in trying to reignite your relationship, ask yourself, "Am I in this alone?" Kate discovered that she wasn't in a relationship with someone who wanted to care about her comfort or include her in activities. Claudia discovered that she had married a person who procrastinated and who thought that problems would evaporate over time.

When we allow others (or ourselves) to disrespect our values and needs, we build resentments. Over time these resentments turn to animosity, annoyance, antagonism, bitterness, exasperation, fury, grudges, outrage, hurt.

How Are You Feeling About Your Relationship?

Circle all that apply.

Happy	Sad	Mad	Glad
Hateful	Bitter	Furious	Hurt
Lonely	Regretful	Depressed	Fearful
Hostile	Boiling	Fuming	Sulky
Indignant	Discouraged	In Despair	Lost
Unsure	Pessimistic	Tense	Alone
Tired	Empty	Dominated	Upset
Hopeful	Crazy	Sad	Tearful

If you don't make some changes, these are the feelings that will dominate you and your relationship. If you decide that you want more in your life than negative feelings and failed attempts to be loved, perhaps it is time to consider leaving.

The Final Try Before Leaving

Can you change your life and still stay in your relationship? Is there any way to problem-solve?

Ross and Bernice

Ross and Bernice's relationship became what they described to be unendingly "painful" and "torturous." Ross found Bernice's constant nagging a trigger for anger. He disliked being around her because she was such a gossip. He admitted that he knew Bernice was a nag and gossip before he married her, but he thought that she would "soften" and "change" when they had a family.

Bernice said that she found Ross to be undependable because he promised to do household chores and never followed through. She said that she found their sex life boring, and that she was a person who had to talk things over with her girlfriends and family because Ross "certainly isn't a problem-solver." Bernice also was repulsed by Ross's lack of hygiene. She was disgusted by the way he smelled because he did not shower enough.

Ross and Bernice had four children by the time they came to see me. They were discussing divorce, but had yet to reach a decision. On a scale of 0 to 10, I had them rate the amount of irritation they caused each other. See below for how they rated their items of discontent.

Ross and Bernice's Irritation Worksheet

Ross's Irritation Ratings with Bernice:

Nagging	10
Gossiping	10
Overspending	6
Micromanaging the kids	5
Personal hygiene	2
Work ethic	0
Behavior when angry	3

Bernice's Irritation Ratings with Ross

Sex life	10
Unreliability	10
Interaction with the kids	0
Inability to problem-solve	9
Personal hygiene	10
Work ethic	9
Anger behavior	10

We discussed the various ways they had tried to solve the issues between them. From their report, it sounded like Ross and Bernice had tried to "prove" their points by making the other person wrong, and therefore confirming and justifying why the other person had to do the changing in order to solve the problem. This method doesn't work.

Here's what happened: Ross and Bernice were supported to begin working on problems by selecting one of the items on their lists that they thought would be fairly uncomplicated to change. They both agreed to work on personal hygiene. Ross admitted that he should shower after playing soccer with his pals. He admitted he was "too lazy." Bernice acknowledged that after a day with the children she was exhausted and taking a shower was the "last thing I want to do before bed." After some discussion, Ross and Bernice agreed each of them would shower every day—even when they didn't want to. Bernice found that she enjoyed being physically near Ross because "he doesn't smell." Ross discovered that he liked feeling clean when he went to bed. Was the problem solved? No, because it had gone on so long. Was this couple diminishing the irritation caused by their personal hygiene habits? Yes! Ross was willing to work to make changes and so was Bernice.

In therapy, we went through item by item that caused irritation. Bernice's desire to leave the marriage diminished. Ross's anger was less often sparked, because he felt he had a partner. The couple was working together to problem-solve. After time, Ross agreed to attend an anger management class. They made a contract about the division of household labor (below). They eventually became sexual again. Bernice did not leave her marriage. She had a husband who had become willing to work on the irritations. They saved their marriage.

Was this a "perfect" progression out of an unhappy romantic relationship? Absolutely not. In fact, Bernice made so much money from Ross's contract violations that she was able to buy the very expensive pair of shoes that she had dreamed about having!

If Ross and Bernice had not been able to work together to attack the irritations between them, this marriage would have ended. One or the other of them would have left.

Could Ross or Bernice have stayed in their URR and lived separate lives?

I asked them, and the answer was a resounding "No!" Why? "Because living with the irritations that turned into periods of demeaning anger weren't good for either one of us or for the children."

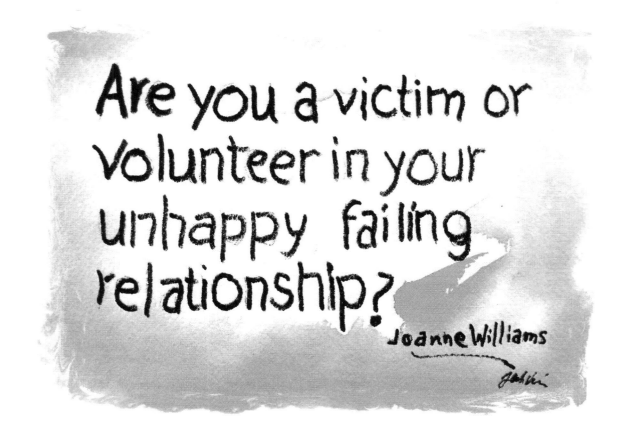

Ross and Bernice's Household Division of Labor Contract

Household Responsibility	Job Description	Consequence for Not Completing This Task
Ross: Every day after work and before 8:00 p.m., clean up Fido's (the dog) droppings and put them in the garbage. Bernice: Will not remind Ross about doing this task.	**Dog Duty Backyard Cleanup** Go to backyard and collect all Fido's droppings, place in a bag, and put in the trash can. Wash off the trowel afterward and put it in the tool shed.	Ross will pay Bernice $5.00 for each time this task is not completed by 8:00 p.m. Bernice: Each time Ross is reminded by Bernice that the task is not done, Bernice will pay Ross $5.00.
Bernice: Will do the family wash twice a week, fold it, and deliver it to the clothes owner's rooms. She will put away her own folded wash. Wash will be done on Wednesdays and Saturdays. Bernice will *not* remind Ross about fulfilling this agreement. Ross: Will put his folded wash away by the time he goes to bed. He will also assist the children in putting away their folded wash before they go to bed.	**Laundry** Bernice is in charge of purchasing all laundry supplies, washing and drying all the family clothes, sheets, etc., folding them, and delivering them to the area in which they belong. Ross is to assist the children who need help with putting away their clean clothes before they go to bed. Those children who are able to take on this responsibility will put their clothes away in the appropriate place before going to bed. Ross will oversee the putting away of clean clothes on Wednesdays and Saturdays.	Bernice will stop doing the wash for seven days from the day Ross doesn't comply with helping his family put their clean clothes away on Wednesday and Saturday. Ross will do the wash for seven days and also be in charge of helping his children put their clean clothes away. If Bernice misses a Wednesday or Saturday wash commitment (without prior agreement) then Bernice will do Ross's commitment for seven days from the day she forgot to do the wash.
Ross: To mow the lawn every Saturday morning by 10:00 a.m. He will leave the trimmings in the lawn mower and put the mower by the	**Lawn Mowing** Ross will mow the lawn on Saturday morning, and when finished he will take the mower over to the organics bin by 11:00 a.m.	If Ross does not mow the lawn by the appointed time, he will have to do Bernice's job for the next two weeks. If Bernice doesn't empty the

organics bin. Bernice: Empty the lawn mower into the organics bin and put the mower back in the garden shed by 11:00 a.m.	Bernice will empty the trimmings into the bin and replace the mower into the garden shed and lock the shed's door. Ross and Bernice agree that they can negotiate on the day this task is to be completed depending on weather and children's activities. This negotiation to be completed by Friday night at 9:00 p.m.	trimmings and return the mower to the garden shed, she will be responsible for mowing the lawn for the next two weeks.
Those children under the age of three are not responsible for clearing their plates from the table. Starting with Ross, he and Bernice will alternate weeks monitoring that dished are in the dishwasher by 9:00 p.m. each night. Each parent may delegate some of this work to children. If delegating to a child, the delegating parent must create a contract with that child so he/she knows exactly what is expected and what the consequences are for noncompliance. Dishwasher is to be turned to "on" after loading it. The parent who is not doing the loading will be in charge of unloading the dishwasher the next day. Again if delegating to a child, a contract must be made with that child.	**Dishes** Ross starts with loading dishwasher by 9:00 p.m. for one week. Bernice unloads dishwasher before she leaves for work and puts away clean dishes for one week. Then they alternate. Neither person is to remind the other party about what time it is.	For every shift missed and for disrespecting the time limit by more than five minutes, a fine of $5.00 is paid to the other party by the person who disrespected this agreement.

In looking at this contract, it might seem picky and complicated. It is. The description of jobs in the "Division of Labor Contract" *needs* to be detailed. The detail leaves little room for misunderstandings. Ross and Bernice decided to address the household responsibilities that they deemed most important. They also selected these items because these were the ones that caused the most contention between them.

After the first month of implementing this contract, Bernice reported that she felt she "might be able to change her opinion about Ross's unreliability." She said that it was "really so hard not to remind Ross of what he was supposed to be doing; I had to bite my tongue."

Ross reported that "the nagging has declined, and I feel better about Bernice because she isn't following me around reminding me to do something." Ross also said that he was feeling more sexual toward Bernice.

Fair Fighting Rules

While in a disagreement or heated dispute we sometimes go for the other person's jugular because we have practiced "winning" arguments. When we engage in winning, it is informative that we ask ourselves, *What do I get when I win?* The answer is usually a resounding *nothing*! You may win by intimidation, but then all you have is a person who agreed due to exhaustion or whom you verbally abused into submission. This strategy doesn't accomplish anything. Go for negotiation, problem-solving, and collaboration!

1. Be sure you identify the *one* reason you are angry.
2. Discuss one item at a time. Do not discuss one issue then another and another. Just one item and then go do something else. Dumping all one's issues in a single discussion is too much.
3. Degrading language is insulting. Discuss the *issue* and *not* the person.
4. Use "I" statements. Resist starting sentences with the accusatory "You."
5. People's attention span is usually eight seconds to 20 minutes![22] Take turns talking and keep it short. One minute is usually the best.
6. Don't refuse to participate in the conversation. This is rude and does not contribute to problem-solving.
7. Do *not* yell! Who shouts the loudest accomplishes nothing.
8. Take a time out if things get too heated. This does not mean just walking out on your partner. This means saying to your partner, "I'm getting a little worked up. I need a break. I'm going for a short walk and I'll be back in ten minutes." Slamming the door on your way out only serves to shut down conversation.

---

[22] Leon Watson, *"Humans Have a Shorter Attention Span Than Goldfish, Thanks to Smartphones," The Telegraph. Science (May 15, 2015).*

9. *Listen*. Most people listen with an agenda. We interrupt the speaker to make our point. This is not listening. Listening is just hearing what someone has to say without comment and saying, "Thank you for telling me that." Take turns listening.

10. Problem-solve. Negotiate. Collaborate.

11. Being so cruel that the other person has no choice but to either fight back or leave is called "hitting below the belt." Decide what the purpose of the argument is. Is it about assassinating your partner's character or is it about problem-solving?

12. Avoid attacking your partner's character, such as telling him/her, "You're neurotic," or "You're depressing."

13. Ask for feedback and clarification. It is important to check out if you heard what you were told correctly. Paraphrase what you heard and request feedback about whether or not you heard it accurately.

14. Follow anger with a clear request for a change.

15. Don't argue while under the influence of a mind-altering substance.

CHAPTER 5

How to Leave My
Unhappy Romantic Relationship

Not everyone
who is single
is lonely.
Not everyone
who is taken
is in love.

Leaving My
Unhappy Romantic Relationship

Before you finally decide to leave your URR, do one last check-in with yourself. Do what I like to call a "Ben Franklin": list the pros and cons of leaving. See "Pros and Cons of Leaving My URR," below, for an example.

One Final Inventory Before You Leave

If you are in a URR in which you have tried everything you can think of to "save" the relationship to no avail, why would you stay?

Are you trying to save your URR all by yourself?
☐ Yes
☐ No

Are you going to continue working on your URR?
☐ Yes
☐ No

Do you have a partner who is also working on your URR?
☐ Yes
☐ No

Are you going to leave?
☐ Yes
☐ No

☐ Maybe

(How long have you been stuck in the "maybe"?)

Does your URR bring you more pain than joy?

☐ Yes

☐ No

Do you live in past memories because the current ones are so painful?

☐ Yes

☐ No

Do you refuse to take no for an answer? (Couples often make promises they have no intention of keeping. Based on these empty promises we hope for change, but none occurs. Believe the behaviors *not* the promises. For example, if you are in a URR with an alcoholic and he/she has promised you that the alcohol use will stop, has it? If behavior changes such as getting treatment, going to AA, getting a recovery sponsor haven't taken place—that is the behavioral "NO!" Believe the behavioral change and not the promise of change.)

☐ Yes

☐ No

Are you feeling emotionally, physically, and/or verbally abused?

☐ Yes

☐ No

Is your partner putting any *real* effort into the relationship?

☐ Yes

☐ No

Do you have fundamentally different values and goals?

☐ Yes

☐ No

Are you depressed about your home life?

☐ Yes

☐ No

Do you imagine a happier life without your partner?

☐ Yes

☐ No

Have you decided that life is too short to spend it crying?

☐ Yes

☐ No

Is it worth it to you to stay in an endurable relationship?

☐ Yes

☐ No

Do you believe that your life is too precious to spend it arguing?
☐ Yes
☐ No

Are your children's lives too valuable to spend with unhappy parents?
☐ Yes
☐ No

Are you saying to yourself, "I can't live this way"?
☐ Yes
☐ No

Is your URR simply not a good match for you?
☐ Yes
☐ No

Is your suffering causing others in your family to suffer also?
☐ Yes
☐ No

By staying in your URR are you also depriving your partner and/or children from living happily?
☐ Yes
☐ No

Are you teaching your children that primary relationships are to be endured rather than to be accepting and loving?
☐ Yes
☐ No

Are your arguments gridlocked?
☐ Yes
☐ No

Are your relationship problems permanent?
☐ Yes
☐ No

Unless optional suffering is a lifestyle to which you have become accustomed, *it's time to leave if most of your responses endorse unhappiness.* If you do decide to leave, you'll begin a new life. You'll have a potential for having a happy romantic relationship. Your children, if any, will live in a less negatively charged environment.

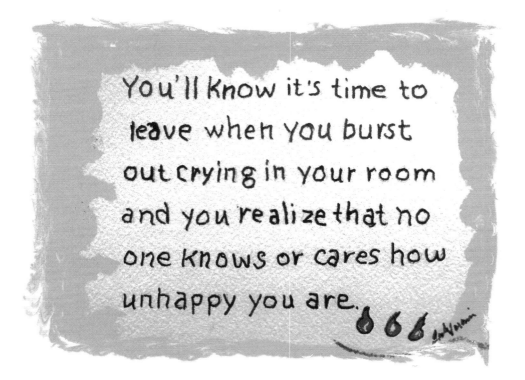

Pros and Cons of Leaving My URR

Below, find an example of a pros and cons list. Following that is a template for you to create your own.

Pros: Reasons to Leave	Cons: Reasons Against Leaving
I can live by myself.	My partner pays half the rent.
I don't have to be criticized.	I will have financial challenges.
My kids don't like my partner.	I will have to hire a sitter.
I can have some peace.	I don't have to keep arguing.

Blank Template

Pros: Reasons to Leave	Cons: Reasons Against Leaving

Statistical Review About Why People Leave URRs

It is really scary to leave a romantic relationship, even if it is unhappy. Now that we have identified how we got ourselves into our URR and the reasons we have stayed in it, let's look at a few statistics about why people really do end their domestic partnerships, marriages, and other types of romantic relationships. While these statistics about the breakdown of relationships are focused on marriages, I have found that they apply across the board and show the reasons for incompatibilities.

Common Factors for Marital Instability[23]

Respondents were asked to select, from a list of 18 options, the factors that contributed to their marriages breaking down.

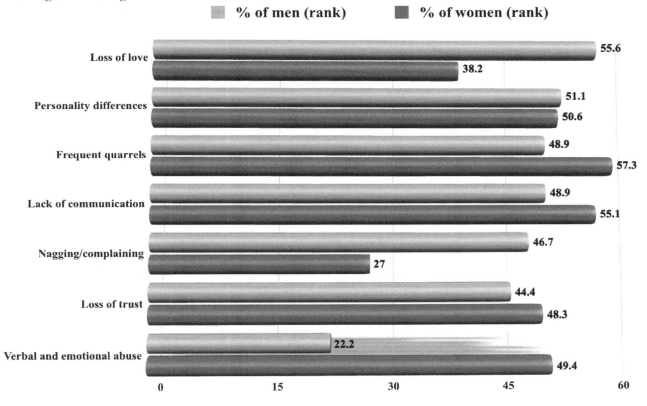

Look at this graph! It shows that 48.9% of men and 57.3% of women have been unable to communicate past their frequent quarrels; 48.9% of men and 55.1% of women leave their relationship due to a lack of communication!

---

[23] *http://rilek1corner.com/2015/11/24/reasons-for-divorces-differ-in-and-out-of-court/.*

Reasons for Wanting a Divorce, by Gender[24]

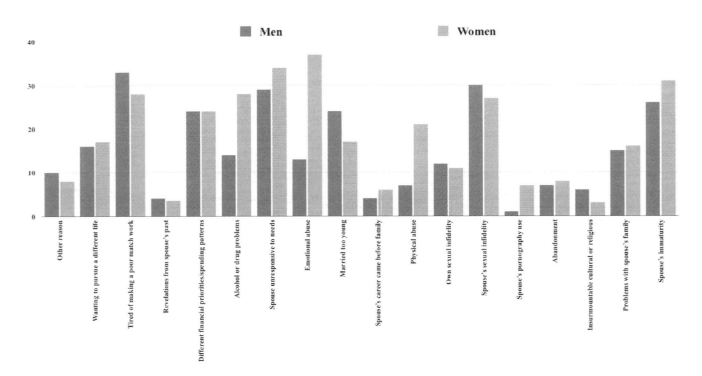

Look at the reasons for wanting a divorce illustrated here. Emotional abuse is the number one reason women want to leave their URR, followed by their spouse not being willing/able to meet their needs. For men, the number one reason for wanting a divorce is being tired of trying to make a poor match work, followed by their spouse's sexual infidelity. Study this chart. Note that *every reason people want a divorce is due to a value violation!*

Despite what anyone says, knowing the statistical reasons for people ending URRs can serve to validate your judgment in deciding to end your unhappy romantic relationship. The statistics can also provide comfort from knowing that you are not alone in your reasoning.

[24] *http://www.austin-institute.org/research/divorce-in-america/.*

Cost of Divorce

Unless you have a history with divorce, many of us in URRs find ourselves stuck due to the unknown. The cost of getting divorced (a litigated divorce with each party having an attorney) in the United States ranges between $10,000 and $20,000 depending on where you live.[25]

We can look at those numbers and say to ourselves, "That is too much money; I can't ever afford that." Here are some other possibilities:[26]

1. Attorneys give one free initial meeting. Go get a few and collect data about what your rights are as both a domestic partner or as a spouse.
2. The do-it-yourself divorce can be complicated. It is the most beneficial for couples who have minimal assets, have been married two to three years, and who don't have children. Hire an attorney to review your documents.
3. Mediation is a way to divorce without paying an attorney to work out all the details. By working with a mediator (who may or may not be an attorney), the divorcing couple works to come to an agreement.
4. Collaborative divorce requires a couple to work out the divorce settlement without going to court. Each party hires his/her own lawyer, whose role is to assist in negotiating a settlement. Once there is an agreement, all parties sign it (including the attorneys); there is usually one meeting in Family Court so a judge can also sign the agreement.
5. Pro bono work (free legal representation) is offered by many attorneys. Make some calls to inquire.
6. FreeAdvice.com and Avvo.com offer free advice!
7. Investigate Legal Aid in your county.

This list in no way is meant to give any reader legal advice. It is meant to create ideas to help break through fears.

There are many ways to leave an unhappy romantic relationship. First, you have to decide just how you want to leave yours. Here are a few ways my patients have reported they left:

1. I waited until my partner was away on a trip and moved everything I wanted into the apartment I rented a month before.

---

[25] *www.divorcestatistics.info/how-much-does-divorce-cost-in-the-usa.html.*
[26] *Jeff Landers, "The Four Divorce Alternatives," Forbes (April 24, 2012),*
https://www.forbes.com/sites/jefflanders/2012/04/24/the-four-divorce-alternatives.

2. After an argument, I packed my things, put the dog in the car, and went to my parents'.

3. I rented a house and in the Realtor's office told my wife that I was leaving her.

4. I told my partner how unhappy I was in the relationship. When she refused to join in that conversation, I told her I was leaving. I moved in with a friend.

5. I called the police and filed a domestic violence report after my husband pushed me onto the sofa and wouldn't let me get up. I filed a restraining order. "And that was that!"

6. I got a free consultation with a lawyer so I would know my rights. I had my husband served at his office. That day I told the kids that Daddy wasn't going to live with us anymore because we didn't know how to communicate well. I took my two kids to the park so the three of us could talk and I could answer any questions they had. I did not answer my cell phone. I had my brother and his good friend come to the house around the time my husband comes home. I took my kids to their grandparent's house to do their homework. My husband was furious. I asked him to leave. He did.

7. I packed up my partner's things in suitcases and boxes while she was on a getaway with her girlfriends. I put them on the front porch. I texted her that our relationship was over and told her to come get her stuff.

8. I took my wife to dinner and told her how unhappy I was and that I wanted to terminate our marriage. She was not surprised. We worked out the details of how and when I would move out and what we would say to our children. We told them together.

9. I was having an affair and my husband found out. We had a knockdown fight, and he stormed away. I was served divorce papers by the end of the week.

There are ways to leave your URR that are filled with integrity and kindness. There are also ways to leave that are dramatic and traumatizing for all involved. Sure it's much easier to have a horrendous battle and walk out, but that way you don't leave with grace. That way you might violate so many of your uncompromisable values that you feel guilty about leaving. Once we decide to leave our URR, we have to plan just how we want to say "goodbye."

Kindly?

Abruptly?

Rudely?

Angrily?

Couldn't care less?

With thought about how not to trigger the worst in you?

In a manner that won't elicit anger and retribution?

In a way that I won't feel bad about later?

With the goal of inflicting emotional pain?

In hopes that you will find a better life?

From the list above, circle all that apply as to just how you want to leave your URR. If you feel that leaving as kindly and painlessly as possible is the way you want to approach your departure, it will require organization.

Organizing My Departure

If you don't care how you leave, read this section anyway. It might change your mind.

If you do care, here are some ideas for how to organize your departure.

1. Make a decision. Review if you have tried everything (couple's therapy, conversations with your partner, etc.), if your partner hasn't tried to work on the relationship, if infidelity has taken place, if you don't make decisions together, if you don't communicate or agree on any topic, if you are dissatisfied with your partner, if you are miserable, if your relationship is abusive and/or if you and your partner have separate interests and friends.
2. Decide not to leave your partner in the heat of the moment. That way you will not say mean things you cannot take back and you will have had time to create a course of action. However, you also have to decide if safety precautions are necessary. No matter how you handle the announcement that you want to end your URR, does your partner have such a temper that you will be in danger? In that case an abrupt departure is in order.
3. Keep the decision to leave to yourself until after you tell your partner. That way the news won't reach your URR before you tell him/her. If you have trusted friends/relatives who can give you advice and who will respect your need for secrecy, tell a select few.
4. Consider how to leave with some financial security. It might take you a few months to plan a financial exit strategy and to put it in place.

5. Create a plan:
- Set up a separate bank account.
- Find a place to live.
- Make copies of documents such as income tax filings, copy your home computer's hard drive, take photos of belongings, bank accounts, etc.
- What to do about the children? Do you want your partner to see the kids anymore? What about school?

6. Contact an attorney or paralegal who specializes in family law. Shop around. The initial visit is usually free. Discuss what your rights are.

7. Create a budget that will include your current financial obligations as well as address financial obligations as the result of ending your URR. Include those areas in which you might have to cut back.

8. Alimony and child support might not be part of your financial future!
- Will your spouse responsibly pay?
- Does your spouse have a job?
- Can you actually count on your spouse?

If you have been the main financial provider, *you* may be the one paying alimony and child support, regardless of gender.

Registered Domestic Partnerships

Make sure you learn about the legal rights in registered domestic partnership dissolutions. They vary from state to state.

For Those Ending an Unhappy Romantic Relationship That Is Not Legally Binding

There are differences between leaving a marriage, leaving a registered domestic partnership (RDP), and leaving a relationship in which you cohabitated. Dissolution of a marriage or an RDP comes with legal guidelines. Leaving a relationship in which one cohabitated can be even more complicated.

Did you purchase property together? What happens to it if you break up?

Do you jointly rent the property you share with your URR? Before you moved in together did you decide what happens if you break up? Do you have this in writing? Be aware of the form "Complaint for Eviction," which you might have to pick up at your local courthouse if you move out and your partner decides not to pay the rent.

Have you written down the inventory of what property you brought into your living arrangement?

Have you kept track of jointly acquired assets and how much each of you contributed to its purchase?

Do you think you are entitled to palimony (financial support and compensation sometimes awarded by one member of an unmarried couple to the other after dissolving their partnership)? Remember, palimony is not a legal term and most unmarried people have no rights to expect support unless they have previously agreed to it.

Have you discussed liability for debts?

After organizing our departure, we now come to the place where we put our feet where our emotions are.

Contract About Organizing My Departure

Agreement	My Responsibilities	Consequences for Breaking Agreements
I have made a decision to leave my URR.	Before leaving I will do research so I am protected from homelessness and financial instability.	Could be forced to return to my URR. Could be homeless. Could be hungry. Could jeopardize custody of my children.
I will plan finances by: Opening a separate checking account. Getting a separate credit card. Make copies of the last five years of tax returns (or however long you have been together) if you have a marriage or domestic partnership.	To follow through on making sure I have some financial solvency. Look for a job. Investigate child care costs. Do research about moving costs and rent.	Leaving with no plan, no money, no home, and no job.
I will do my legal research by: Contacting three attorneys for a free initial consultation about my rights. I will discuss alimony and child support as applicable.	After these consultations I will make a budget for myself to see how much money I will need. I will explore where I can cut costs.	Not knowing your legal rights and leaving your URR in ignorance about your future.
I will review this plan with one trusted friend who I am sure will respect my need for privacy.	I will take my friend's feedback about this contract into serious consideration.	I will only be relying on myself. In these situations it is often comforting to have some support.

Telling Your URR You Are Leaving

After organizing the departure we now come to the place where we put our feet where our emotions are. You have now made a decision to leave. You have made the monumental decision that you would be happier if you weren't with your partner anymore. You have decided just how you want to leave. You have organized your departure. Now what?

If you are like most people, this is often the most anxiety-ridden, scary, and sad part of leaving your URR. How can I tell my URR I'm leaving? That is the question.

If you have decided to leave your URR with dignity, it is important to decide and perhaps practice what you are going to say. Decide on a time and place where the two of you can be alone. Never break up via text or the phone. Tell a trusted friend about your plans. (If your URR has been an abusive one, having a private conversation is out of the question. Safety is the only thing you should consider. This is addressed in the next section.)

In your conversation provide your soon-to-be-ex partner the main reason (one reason, not an entire list of past grievances) that you find yourself unable to continue on in the URR. No matter his/her reaction, be calm. One of the most challenging things about breaking up with URRs who trigger negative feelings is not to take any of the hooks that triggered our emotions in the past.

Remember, you are *leaving* and not just taking a break! If you phrase your departure as "taking a break," you are giving your URR hope for a continued relationship bond.

Listen to your URR. Listen to what he/she has to say. Listening does not require any interaction from you. All it requires is listening and then saying, "Thank you for telling me that." Period! Be sure to accept responsibility for your mistakes. You do *not* have to defend or explain. Just listen.

Discuss your plans for moving out. Discuss what you would like to take with you. Share your timeline. Be ready for tears, begging, blaming, promises, threats, etc. Be ready for anger, yelling, name calling. Be sure *you* do not engage in any of these behaviors. If you feel that a break in this discussion is necessary, take one. Arrange to meet in a public place if your URR's emotions are too volatile.

Then—*break up*! The relationship is over! Done! It is time to heal and to establish your own home—your own happy nest and your own stuff, in peace.

The "I'm Leaving You" Conversation Checklist

☐ I have made my decision to leave my URR.

☐ I have scheduled a time and place to meet in private.

☐ I have made an outline of what I would like to say.

☐ My main reason for leaving this URR is _____. I will stay on topic and not bring up other resentments.

☐ I plan to be honest.

☐ I plan to listen and not interject my opinion or feedback into anything my URR says. I will stay on topic.

☐ I am able to accept and admit that I too have made mistakes in this URR. I will apologize but I will not explain or justify myself.

☐ I am ready for my URR's negative response, but I hope that he/she will eventually see the wisdom of this parting.

☐ I have written out my moving schedule. I have made a copy for my URR.

☐ I have written out a list of items I would like to take with me. I have made a copy for my URR.

☐ I have informed _____ when and where I will be advising my URR that I will be leaving the URR. She/he will call me every hour.

☐ I have made arrangements to stay _____ when this conversation is done.

☐ I will be moving to _____.

Add anything else you think you need to complete the process of leaving your URR. *Leave as you would like to be left!*

Leaving an Abusive URR

If you have been in an abusive relationship, you must create a very safe and secret way to leave in order to protect yourself and perhaps your children and family pets. One way to learn how to plan leaving your abusive URR is to contact organizations that help protect victims of domestic abuse and/or violence. Do *not* leave your URR without a plan and without assistance. The National Domestic Violence Hotline regarding domestic violence is 1.800.799.SAFE (7233). This is a confidential hotline that provides assistance.

It is crucial that when leaving an abusive URR you plan ahead. The success of leaving depends on thorough planning. Here are some guidelines:

1. Collect important documents including phone numbers, birth certificates, green cards, etc.
2. Open a bank account without your URR's knowledge. Save some money to be used for emergencies.
3. Use a public computer to search for a job. Libraries are a good place to do research.
4. Sell jewelry or other valuables so you will have extra funds.
5. Open a post office box.
6. Purchase a prepaid cell phone or use a friend's to contact a domestic violence shelter. Ask them for services they provide. Inquire about housing options. Ask for a list of what to take such as medications for you and/or your children or house pets (if applicable).
7. Take photos of injuries that are a result of abuse.
8. Be objective and detached. Be consistent.

The psychology of abusive relationships deserves its own chapter, but is not the topic of this book. Get some education about the cycle of violence, why people stay in them, and the pros and cons of procuring a restraining order. Whatever you do, *be safe*!

The Leaving Script

Many of my patients have come to me saying they have organized their departure, are ready to leave their URR, but they remain stumped about exactly what to say. Jody came to me for help with practicing what she wanted to say to Todd. Here is the script that Jody refined over time. She had great success with it, and her relationship with Todd ended with mutual respect.

Jody and Todd

Jody and Todd were not married. They had lived together for five years when Jody came to see me. She recounted a history full of criticism and an unequal division of community jobs because "Todd expects me to be a maid." Jody said that she had decided to leave her relationship with Todd because "he is all about himself and won't even try to solve problems between us." Jody was sure she wanted to leave her relationship because "I am unhappier than I am happy, and that is no way to live."

Jody was not employed. Todd had supported her for the last five years. Before she met Todd, Jody had been a waitress at a high end restaurant. She and Todd had no children, but they did share a Golden Retriever, Walt, whom they treated like their child.

By the time we met to discuss what Jody was planning to say to Todd about leaving him, she had completed most of the worksheets provided in this book. She had concluded that when she entered into a relationship with Todd, she had been wearing rose-colored glasses and was "in denial about his drinking." She identified the cognitive distortions of minimizing what a negative effect Todd's drinking and marijuana smoking had on their relationship. She blamed his addictive behaviors for her unhappiness. Jody believed that Todd should not drink, and she got angry when he did. She stayed in the relationship because she believed that if she left, Todd would never let her see Walt again.

Walt

Over time, Jody began to recognize that she felt imprisoned in the relationship by her cognitive distortions: minimizing, blame, catastrophizing, and expecting Todd to change because she wanted him to (the control fallacy). She also recognized that she had allowed Todd to violate her values and in the process, she had violated them herself. She identified that her values about balance, contribution, cooperation, personal growth, responsibility, respect, and spirituality had been disregarded. Her mirror neurons enabled her to instinctively understand that she and Todd no longer even liked each other.

Working with her own fears, distortions, and stuck points, she created a formula of what she had been expecting Todd to do to make her happy.

"If Todd would stop drinking, contribute more to house chores, take responsibility for the mean way in which he treats me, and work on living a spiritually centered life, I would be happy." Jody concluded that there was nothing in their relationship that would lead her to believe that Todd had any desire to make substantial changes in the behaviors that were not a match for Jody's. Jody decided that she did not want to continue suffering in her URR.

JODY: Todd, I need about five minutes of your time tomorrow morning. Could you spare that?

TODD: Oh God, is this another lecture?

JODY: No, it's not.

TODD: So what's it about?

Notice the hook to get Jody to satisfy his curiosity.

JODY: Is 8:00 a.m. OK?
TODD: Yeah, yeah, sure. Whatever. What's it about this time?
JODY: I have to go. I won't be home until much later. Bye.

Notice that Jody set a time and that was all she did. She masterfully avoided being hooked into getting into discussions about the topic of the meeting. Then she left the house for the day. She did not return home until 9:00 p.m. and Todd was already passed out in bed.

The next morning, Jody brought Todd some coffee in bed.

JODY: Are you awake enough to give me five minutes?
TODD (drowsily, and assuming a posture of boredom): Yeah. What's on your mind?
JODY: We've been together five years and Todd, I'm very unhappy, and I think you are too. I have made plans to move out. I will be moving next week. I think this is the best for both of us. I know you have been suffering just as much as I have. The main reason I'm leaving is I don't like alcohol and marijuana as much as you do.

Jody has made plans. She has organized her departure. She included Todd's feelings and did not make one accusatory remark about how she thought Todd failed her expectations. She did not point out his unwillingness to change, his drinking, or any other faults. Jody created her leaving script to take into account Todd's feelings as well as her own.

TODD: What? How could you do this? You are just up and leaving? What a bitch! You are just a controlling bitch. Go ahead. Move out. Get the hell out!
JODY: I can see that you are upset, Todd. I'm very surprised. I need to go to the gym and then on to work. I'll see you later.

Examine this conversation. Jody set boundaries, announced her plan in a very empathic manner. She did not enter into a defensive conversation when Todd called her a bitch. Jody kept her cool and then left Todd to his own feelings. Jody was respectful. Also notice that Jody did not ask if she could take Walt or advise Todd about what she would be taking with her. When someone is angry, that is not the time to try to negotiate the material breakup.

That night at home:

TODD (in a very depressed voice): I see you're home. Can't we talk about this? I'm so sorry. I didn't realize you were so upset. I promise I'll try to cut down on drinking and smoking weed. I promise I'll try to treat you better. Please don't leave. I don't know what I'll do if you leave.

Tempting to want to believe the promises that have all been made before without follow-through. Tempting to want to save Todd from his feelings. Tempting to want to make it "all right" for Todd.

JODY: I'm happy to listen to anything you have to say, Todd.

Jody gracefully gave Todd the space to say whatever he wanted to tell her. Jody did NOT engage in trying to solve Todd's issues.

TODD (attempting to manipulate feelings of empathy from Jody): I know it's all my fault. I guess I'm just a bad guy. I can't get over the way I was raised—you know in a family of alcoholics. I don't know any other way.

Todd is not taking any responsibility for his drinking or his behavior. He is blaming others.

JODY: I know you've had a difficult childhood, Todd.

TODD: But you can't imagine how hard it was. You came from a much better family. I never had a good role model. You got all the benefits of two parents, going to school. If you leave me, how will you support yourself? Where will you live? Remember, babe, I've done all that for you.

Todd is trying to induce guilt in pointing out that he came from an unhealthy family whereas she came from a family that had more love and kindness within it. Todd is also using Jody's fears—no job, no housing—to manipulate her to stay.

JODY: I remember, Todd. You have been very generous.

Jody is not explaining or defending herself—she is listening in a kind way.

TODD: Well, if you think you are taking Walt with you, you are way off track. Poor Walt. He is so attached to you.

Todd played his royal flush hand in this poker game of manipulation.

JODY: Yes, Walt will suffer.

Now is not the time to negotiate custody of Walt. It is not the time to negotiate anything. It is the time to listen—only listen. Why? Because Todd is not actually interested in hearing anything Jody has to say—in fact, he's heard it all before. Todd is trying to get his way and that's all. Notice he has not offered one thing that he would be willing to do in order to change any of the relationship dynamics that don't work for either one of them.

TODD: And that's all you have to say? Well, fine. I'm going out!

Todd leaves with a slam to the door.

How do you think Jody is doing so far?
Has she resisted manipulation and guilt?
Has she maintained politeness?
Has she successfully combated any need to comfort Todd and thus put herself off track?
Was she kind?
Did she take some of the responsibility for the relationship not being a match?
Did she refuse to take any of the "hooks" that Todd presented to engage her in an argument?

Jody has been well rehearsed, and she is sticking to the script. She started packing her things. She spent time with Walt. She felt sad and a little scared. She kept herself focused on her decision to leave her URR. She practiced a mantra: *This is the very best thing you could ever do for you and for Todd.*

The next morning was a Saturday. Jody knew that Todd had returned home in a drunken stupor. She took Walt for a walk. She was sipping coffee when Todd came downstairs to join her:

TODD: I see you've started packing.
JODY: Yes, I started last night.
TODD: Where are you going?
JODY: I have rented a room with a friend.
TODD: Who?
JODY: Her name is Nancy. You don't know her. I used to work with her at the restaurant.
TODD: And just how are you going to pay for that?
JODY: I got a job.

Jody's departure organization is really paying off. She has freed herself from her greatest fears—being homeless with no money. Notice how Todd has played on those fears.

TODD: Doing what? What can you do? You haven't worked in five years 'cuz you've been living off me!

It is tempting to remind Todd that for the last five years she has been cooking, cleaning, taking care of Walt since he was a puppy....

JODY: I got a job at a restaurant.

Jody is being respectful, kind, and gracious. She is not responding to any of Todd's put-downs.

TODD: Where?

Todd is displaying interest in every detail.

JODY: Todd, I am so grateful for your concerns. I will be OK. Really I will. I'm going to go meet Nancy now and take some of my packed boxes with me. I'll probably be back around 9:00 p.m.

Jody has deflected his question and has planned her day so she won't be around his inquiries or his moods.

Jody returned at 8:00. Todd had been drinking. Jody felt that she might be verbally attacked if she continued to stay in the house.

JODY: I'm going to visit my sister. I might spend the night. I'll see you tomorrow.

Jody has really taken care of herself. She has made a safety plan for where to go if she is feeling uncomfortable being around Todd. On Sunday, she completed packing her personal items. She gave Todd a list of the things she would be taking with her. She asked him for his feedback. She told Todd that even though they had purchased their bed together, there was a bed at the other house so she wanted him to keep the bed. Then she brought up Walt.

JODY: Any questions or objections to the stuff on the list?
TODD: Whatever.
JODY: Then I'll have my sister and brother-in-law here next Saturday at 10:00 to get the items on the list. Does that time work for you?
TODD: No.
JODY: What time will work for you?
TODD: No time.

Right there is a tremendous opportunity to engage in a horrible argument. There will be no winners.

JODY: Todd, I know you're upset. I hope you can admit that neither of us has been happy for a long time. We are just different. I hope you will give me a time that is convenient for you. Text me.
TODD: Whatever.
JODY: One more thing, Todd. You know I love Walt. Can we share him?
TODD: No!

There is absolutely nothing Jody can say to this. Time to leave. Time to feel her emotions in another setting.

JODY: That makes me sad. I hope you will reconsider. I wish you well, Todd.

How many invitations to have a knockdown battle did Jody resist? She left with integrity and grace. She left with dignity. She left without insulting Todd or making him the "bad guy."

In session, Jody felt empowered by the way she had handled this breakup. She grieved her loss of Walt. She identified that leaving Walt was the saddest and most difficult part of her departure. We discussed if she should call Todd to see if he had changed his mind or if it would be better for her to sever all ties. Jody decided on the latter.

The next topic for Jody to address was how to recover from her URR. What should she do to get through each day? Should she act on any urges to call Todd? What would be her plan when euphoric recall (memories of the "good times") flooded her thoughts?

Recovery from Leaving Your Unhappy Romantic Relationship

Now what do we do to get ourselves through all the feelings and fears that come from actually leaving an unhappy romantic relationship? After a breakup the brain tends to teeter-totter between positive and negative memories. On one hand our mind focuses on all the negatives that led to our departure. On the other hand our mind remembers those soft and loving experiences we had with our ex. We often experience that push-and-pull of urges to return to our ex or to continue on with our leaving the relationship plans.

Memories

The more emotionally significant a memory is, the more likely it to be remembered. In the process of memory storage in the brain, positive and negative aspects tend to be enhanced. Negative memories include more item-specific visual details, such as someone hitting our arm. Positive memories tend to have more sensorial and contextual details, such as recalling that starry night in which we got the first kiss from our ex. There are no "flashbulb" memories that contain the exact details of an event. Most memories are incomplete. They tend to omit detail and context. So, even though we think we have picture-perfect memories of events, we do not. What we do have are memories of the emotions/feelings that have been stored in the amygdala that are related to an event.

When leaving a URR, there is a propensity to have some euphoric recall. That is, there are impulses to remember past events in a positive light and overlook the negative. We remember the hot makeup sex after an argument. Often we don't remember what the argument was all about, but we do engage in memories of the sensual contact afterward. If we direct our concentration toward euphoric recall, the urge to call your ex, see your ex, or move back in with your ex will haunt you. This is self-induced suffering based on a sensory memory. When leaving your URR, there is also a tendency to spotlight the negative. This only serves to stir up uncomfortable and angry emotions. When we engage either in positive or negative memories we are living in the past—not in the present.

Let's not forget the strong emotion of grief—grief that you no longer have a partner, grief that you will likely not see the friends who were enjoyed as a couple, sadness that you feel like an island without a history that a romantic partner knows, feelings of loss of a loving bond, and so on. Let yourself feel grief but don't make it your "date" for the day.

The day you leave your URR, you begin an adjustment period. Try to make this as pleasant as possible. If you have organized your departure, you will have a new room, apartment, or house that needs to be made into *your* nest. Make sure you get enough exercise and sleep. Eat healthy meals. Honor your courage. After all, you exited with integrity: you did not deliberately make life miserable for your partner, you did not use pets/children as pawns in a power play. If you followed the advice in this book, you did not start an affair—this would only add more pain, suffering, and guilt to your departure. You didn't avoid the "I'm leaving you" conversation and you did not pack your bags and disappear. Hooray for you! If you left because you *are* having an affair, go back and read this book from the beginning!

Let's explore the steps for recovering from leaving your URR:

1. Resist the urge to dissect the relationship. Reminiscing, blaming yourself, doing the "what ifs" and "what could I have done betters" might be useful at some period later on, but doing it right after your breakup will only make the changes you are trying to embrace more difficult.

2. Contextualize your relationship. Once you thought you knew the person you were with, but over time, he/she turned into a stranger or perhaps even an adversary. You left a person who was not a match for you. You left a person who didn't share your values and who violated them. You left a person who brought suffering into the relationship. The time to analyze your relationship is not now!

3. Believe that you are smarter and more resilient that you ever thought you were.

4. Focus on loving the person staring back at you in the mirror.

5. Make a list of benefits that you have from leaving your URR.

6. Allow yourself to cry.

7. Fill the hole. How?
   - Practice visualizations.
   - Say positive affirmations like:
     o My life is full of play and humor.
     o My life is courageous and free.
     o I have a good heart.
   - Listen to meditation CDs.
   - Get something cuddly—a stuffed or live "pet."
   - Call friends.
   - Watch uplifting YouTube presentations.
   - Make jewelry or develop a hobby.
   - Enjoy your trip to the grocery store.
   - Develop a spiritual practice—if you have made your URR your "higher power" it is imperative that you get a new source of inspiration and comfort.
   - Write a gratitude list before bed.
   - Go on vacation either alone or with a friend.
   - Exercise—join a gym and if possible, get an exercise partner; go for hikes and appreciate nature.
   - Get enough sleep: you might want to download Mindifi apps for sleep and relaxation.

- Read some self-help books—but not too many! *Getting Past Your Breakup: How to Turn a Devastating Loss into the Best Thing That Ever Happened to You* by Susan J. Elliott, *It's Called a Breakup Because It's Broken: The Smart Girl's Break-Up Buddy* by Greg Behrendt and Amiira Ruotola-Behrendt, and/or *The Break Up Manual for Men: How to Recover from a Serious Break Up* by Andrew Ferebee could be helpful.

8. Engaging in counseling has been a source of enlightenment and comfort for many of us coming from URRs.
9. Set goals.
10. Create balance in your new life. Frantic activity to avoid grieving is exhausting. Make your life simple because leaving a URR is like taking on an additional full-time job—you have to continuously work on it.

Don't forget the practicalities of your breakup:

1. Breakup digitally—change your Facebook page, unfriend people who have not actually been real friends.
2. Get your name off leases, jointly held bills, credit cards, etc.
3. Apply for your own credit card.
4. Delete your name from joint bank accounts.
5. Advise your relatives about your breakup. This can raise problems if your family was "in love" with your URR. Sometimes family members side with the URR and not with their relative who left the relationship. Prepare yourself for this possibility. It will show you which of your family members are loyal to you and love you unconditionally. If this happens it could be really painful. You must consider it useful information about who is not in your corner. It is not useful to try to convince your family members about "what a schmuck" your URR was. *You* know how you feel. Defending, explaining, trying to convince is simply an energy drain. Place your attention elsewhere.
6. If you are the one to tell the mutual friends that you and your URR hung around with, don't demonize your URR. Don't process your feelings with them. Preserve your dignity and self-esteem.
7. Change car registrations.
8. If there are personal items that still need to be removed from the residence you shared with your URR, arrange for someone else to get them.

ONE OF THE MOST COURAGEOUS
DECISIONS YOU'LL EVER MAKE
IS TO FINALLY LET GO OF WHAT IS
HURTING YOUR HEART AND SOUL.

Jody's Breakup Recovery Contract

Agreement	My Responsibilities	Consequences for Breaking Agreements
I will not call Todd. I will only text to make arrangements about Walt or picking up my items.	For six months I will not engage in reminiscing about the relationship or dissecting it with Todd. Then I will decide if I want to discuss it.	I open myself to the temptation to be pulled back into a URR.
Exercise three times a week. Walk with Walt two times a week.	To help my body produce the endorphins that will help me feel happy.	Depression Sadness Time to think about the URR
I will read one self-help book about breaking up with a long-term relationship.	To provide my brain with new information.	Shutting myself off to new ideas and ways of thinking about my relationship with Todd.
Keep myself surrounded by *only* supportive friends and relatives.	Go out to dinner, have people over, do Meetup.com with people who are supportive.	Opening myself up to criticism, doubt, seeking approval, and putting my feelings last.

What About Walt?

About one week after Jody left Todd, Todd texted Jody to tell her that Walt wasn't eating and he wondered if he could drop Walt off for a visit. It was very tempting to immediately pick up the phone and jump into that opportunity. Jody was wise. She called a few trusted friends. She arranged for Todd to take Walt to one of her pal's where Jody would pick him up after Todd had left. Walt was going to spend the weekend with Jody! She was elated! Jody's heart lightened. Walt started eating! Currently, that arrangement still exists. Walt spends weekends with Jody and Todd still drops him over at Jody's friend's home and picks him up there as well.

Jody and Todd haven't seen each other in five months. Todd was a very kind and thoughtful person to place his ego aside and put the welfare of Walt first. Not all exes are like that. Sometimes we have to start over and let adored pets go. If we don't it will become a never-ending power struggle between you and your ex. Be free!

Let's turn our attention to aspirations! Let's examine what healthy relationships are, and how people have sustained happiness in their romantic relationships. Do you want to have a healthy romantic relationship?

CHAPTER 6

Healthy Romantic Relationships

It took me a long time to learn the difference between working on a **healthy relationship** and wasting my time on a long goodbye. Never again!

STEVE MARABOLI

Remember Cinderella? Recall Snow White and the seven dwarfs? What about Sleeping Beauty or *Ever After* with Drew Barrymore? *Crazy, Stupid, Love? 500 Days of Summer?*

Here's the story line: Two people meet. One of them dreams about the other or sees the other and falls instantly in love. Some unexpected barrier keeps them apart. The barrier miraculously gets removed and they get together and live happily ever after! Translation: If you fall in love (lust) with a total and complete stranger, you'll live happily ever after! Really? *Not!* A question for the guys is, when you fall in love with a complete stranger—do you think she will be hot forever? Yes? *Not!* For the women, do you think the stranger you fell for will be kind, thoughtful, romantic, financially solvent? Yes? Maybe *not!* For those with other than heterosexual propensities, do you also think that the stranger you are with will be just right for you over time? Healthy relationships are not created from hooking up with strangers.

I looked at the above paragraph and wondered, am I out of touch? Have I not kept up with the times? In this 21st century, is the idea of "love at first embrace" still going on? No matter your sexual orientation, do we really expect that falling in love with a stranger will lead to long-term happiness? (Dear reader—you might want to review limerence and the "love cocktail" section found in Chapter 1.)

Research

Here's what some of the research says about happy romantic relationships that last:

1. Research from a University of Michigan study published in the *Psychology of Popular Media Culture* journal concluded that watching romantic "love finds a way" movies wherein love overcomes all obstacles creates that belief for viewers. Those who watched TV marriage-themed reality shows also tended to believe in idealized "love at first sight."[27]

However, that same research study also found that those who watched TV sitcoms in which couples have arguments don't endorse "perfect love." They hold more negative views of marriage and committed relationships.

I guess we could summarize that your view of "perfect love" depends on what you watch at the movies or on TV.

2. Research from the University of Washington by Dr. John Gottman addressed how physiology could identify the relationship "masters" and the relationship "disasters."[28] Dr. Gottman and his research team brought newlyweds into their lab, hooked them up to electrodes, and measured their heart rates, blood flow, and how much sweat they produced. These same couples were interviewed six years later. While the "disasters," who were chronically unhappy or had broken up, looked calm, their heart rates, blood flow, and sweat production suggested that each member of the couple was ready to be attacked. They were aggressive toward each other. In contrast, those successful in their relationships, the "masters," showed low physiological arousal; they behaved in a warm and affectionate manner even when they disagreed.

---

[27] *Taryn Hillin, "How Movies and TV Shows Are Changing the Way You Think About Love," The Huffington Post (June 18, 2014), http://www.huffingtonpost.com/2014/06/18/love-study-_n_5508965.html.*
[28] *See John Gottman in References.*

Further investigation in this study showed that when one member of the couple invited a response from the other member, the manner in which the response was delivered had a great influence on the relationship. If a response was provided in a kind and generous manner in which interest was shown and support was provided, people in the relationship felt valued and tended to scan their environment and their partner for things they could appreciate. On the other hand, if a response contained contempt, criticism, and hostility, the love that was between them at one time was killed, and the people in the relationship tended to scan their environment and their partner for mistakes. Thus, over time, the criticized partner felt invisible and worthless.

Gottman concluded that what is brought into the relationship will be a major factor in determining its success: is there kindness and generosity or contempt, criticism, and hostility? He also found that relationship "masters" tended to scan their environment and their partner for things they could appreciate and say thank you for. The "disasters" scanned their environment and their partner for mistakes. This damaged the relationship by making their partner feel unseen and insignificant. Those couples who gave each other the cold shoulder by delivering minimal responses felt unvalued.

This research found that *kindness* is the major predictor of satisfaction and stability in long-term happy relationships. Kindness is the higher path *no matter what*!

I guess we could conclude that looking for positives and being responsive and kind will help create a healthy and happy romantic relationship.

3. Research from Gable, Gonzaga, and Strachman (2006) found that shared joy was another important component in happy relationships. Showing interest and wholeheartedly engaging in your partner's successes creates a bonding opportunity over good news. Gable named this "active-constructive responding." She described it as the act of (stopping what you are doing and) "turning toward" your partner's share of good news by asking questions about it, being interested in the details.[29]

I guess we could conclude that being happy for and interested in your partner's successes will help create a happy romantic relationship.

---

[29] *Shelly L. Gable et al., "Will You Be There for Me When Things Go Right? Supportive Responses to Positive Event Disclosures," Journal of Personality and Social Psychology 91 No. 5 (2006).*

A joy that's shared is a joy doubled.

4. Research from the University of Denver's Center for Marital and Family Studies suggests that having fun together and keeping the relationship interesting, novel, and playful is of paramount importance.[30] The research adds to findings published in 2000 that discovered that couples who participate in exciting and novel activities are happier in their relationship.[31]

I guess we could conclude that doing fun activities together helps cement a happy relationship.

5. Research published in *Human Brain Mapping* found that mirror neurons play an important part in a sustained happy relationship. This research found that in happy long-term relationships displays of *positive emotion* from one's partner activate mirror-neuron activity.[32]

I guess we could conclude that long-term relationship satisfaction is highly influenced by sensitivity to our partner's positive emotion.

---

[30] *Howard Markman, director of the CMFS, and co-director Scott Stanley in as yet unpublished research, cited in Sharon Jayson's "Married Couples Who Play Together Stay Together," USA Today (July 16, 2008),*
https://usatoday30.usatoday.com/news/nation/2008-07-15-fun-in-marriage_n.htm.

[31] *Arthur Aron et al., "Couples' Shared Participation in Novel and Arousing Activities and Experienced Relationship Quality," Journal of Personality and Social Psychology 78 No. 2 (February 2000).*

[32] *Raluca Petrican et al., "Neural Activity Patterns Evoked by a Spouse's Incongruent Emotional Reactions When Recalling Marriage-Relevant Experiences," Human Brain Mapping 36 No. 2 (October 2015).*

6. Research from the *Journal of Sex and Marital Therapy* found that 54% of men and 42% of women in long-term relationships were unhappy with the frequency of sex.[33] Further investigation reported in the *Journal of Personality and Social Psychology* indicates that those who have sex at least once a week find greater relationship satisfaction.[34] The article referred to is titled "Money, Sex, and Happiness: An Empirical Study," and it estimates that increasing sexual activity from once a month to once a week was the equivalent of getting paid an extra $50,000 per year!

I guess we could conclude that having sex at least once a week increases relationship satisfaction substantially.

7. Believe it or not, research indicates that for couples *without* children, long-term relationships are more satisfying! Researchers from the General Social Survey, the National Longitudinal Survey of Youth, and the Survey of Marital Generosity all found that not having a child rendered happier relationships. Regardless of gender orientation or level of income, having a child changes the couple's relationship and negatively alters satisfaction.[35]

I guess we could conclude that long-term relationship satisfaction is higher with couples who decide not to have children.

However, the same research also noted that if a couple does decide to have a child/children five qualities are necessary to help offset the extra work a child requires:

- Sexual satisfaction
- Commitment
- Delivering small acts of kindness to each other, such as making coffee, expressing affection, and being willing to forgive
- Having a good attitude toward raising kids
- Social support from family and friends.

I guess we could conclude that long-term relationship happiness is better when a couple does not have children, but there are also ways to have long-term satisfaction with children in the family.

According to the Center for Parenting Education, research further indicates that if a couple does have a family, it is healthier for the relationship when each partner is in agreement with the other about parenting.[36] Children are masters at "divide and conquer" to get their way. For example, when the answer is "no" from Dad, many kids then go to Mom, who says "yes" without checking with her partner. What often happens is the child takes the "yes" answer and the parents end up arguing about

---

[33] A. Smith et al., "Sexual and Relationship Satisfaction among Heterosexual Men and Women: The Importance of Desired Frequency of Sex," *Journal of Sex and Marital Therapy* 37 No. 2 (2011).

[34] David G. Blanchflower and Andrew J. Oswald, "Money, Sex and Happiness: An Empirical Study," *The Scandinavian Journal of Economics* 106 No. 3 (September 2004).

[35] http://stateofourunions.org/.

[36] "Partners in Parenting," The Center for Parenting Education, http://centerforparentingeducation.org/library-of-articles/focus-parents/partners-parenting-working-together-team/.

what should have been done. Have a "parenting style" conversation *before* you decide to bring a child into the world. An article in *Parenting Today* (based on research by Diana Baumrind) sums this up:[37]

There are basically three main styles of parenting:

1) Authoritarian: The rules are the rules are the rules. No exceptions.
2) Authoritative: This is what I refer to as a "benevolent dictatorship." There are rules, and kids can give their input, but the parents have the final say.
3) Lenient or "laissez-faire": There are minimal rules.

If the two of you don't agree on a parenting style, you need to talk. Also, if you differ on whether your children should be spanked or not—you need to talk.

You may have each grown up with different parenting styles—and we each tend to parent the same way we were parented. If you don't have kids yet but are thinking about it, you must, must, must have this conversation with your partner.

I guess we could advise that having similar parenting styles increases relationship satisfaction in RR.

8. Research published in *The Forum for Family and Consumer Issues* found that financial compatibility is a key component of successful marriages and long-term relationships. They discovered that financial compatibility fosters validation, freedom, power, respect, security, and happiness.[38]

Research from a 2003 survey showed that 93% of the couples in this study (in Utah) indicated finances were a major reason for conflict.[39]

I guess we could conclude that happy long-term relationships involve some agreement about who is going to earn the money (one or both), how it will be spent, who will manage the bill paying responsibilities, when it is OK to use credit to make purchases, and the amount of monthly income to be saved.

---

[37] *Stephanie Sarkis, PhD, "Here, There, and Everywhere: 7 Keys to a Healthy and Happy Relationship," Psychology Today (January 2, 2012), https://www.psychologytoday.com/blog/here-there-and-everywhere/201201/7-keys-healthy-and-happy-relationship.*

[38] *Carolyn Washburn and Darlene Christensen, "Financial Harmony: A Key Component of Successful Marriage Relationship, The Forum for Family and Consumer Issues (2008), https://ncsu.edu/ffci/publications/2008/v13-n1-2008-spring/Washburn-Christensen.php.*

[39] *D. G. Schramm et al., "Marriage in Utah: 2003 Baseline Statewide Survey on Marriage and Divorce," Utah Department of Workforce Services (2003).*

9. Know how to resolve conflict! While there will be conflicts in every romantic relationship, knowing how to argue, collaborate, and negotiate is paramount in sustaining a long-term RR. According to research by John Gottman, it's how you resolve conflict that matters most.[40] Exhibiting contempt, criticizing, being defensive, and stonewalling are *not* ways to resolve conflict. Let's examine what we mean by these four barriers to conflict resolution:

Criticism involves attacking someone's personality or character. If grievances are not resolved they evolve into a long list of complaints about how the other person is somehow failing.

Contempt is the intent to insult your partner's self-esteem. When a partner name calls, uses hostile humor, mocks, sneers, or rolls their eyes, the message is one of "my admiration for you has left" and because you are "inferior" and I am "superior," there is really no need for further conversation.

Defensiveness is a response to contempt that tends to escalate conflict. Defensiveness is evident when a partner denies responsibility, makes excuses, makes assumptions by mindreading and ascribing negative intent to their partner, cross complains (answers their partner's complaint with one of their own), and repeats one's own position over and over without taking into consideration the other's point of view.

Stonewalling occurs when one member of a relationship stops responding and shuts the other out. Stonewalling is a sign that negative thoughts about one's partner have been cemented, and indicates that the RR is in desperate need of change if it is to survive.

Research indicates that learning how to calm oneself assists in preventing the avoidance of necessary conversations and unproductive arguing. Those in happy long-term relationships have learned to

---

[40] *See John Gottman in References.*

listen, have learned to express understanding for their partner's point of view and have acquired methods for preventing "I statement" negativity from taking over their relationship. They do this by telling their partner what's going on with them in the moment using "I statements."

According to Dr. Gottman, there needs to be five times as much positive feeling and interaction between partners as there is negative. See "Fair Fighting Rules" in Chapter 4.

I guess we could conclude that long-term relationship happiness is sustained when the couple has had many conversations about how to collaborate, negotiate, and solve grievances. Perhaps we could also conclude that for each disagreement we need to have five positive interactions to compensate and offset negativity.

10. In his research conducted at Cornell University about how fundamental differences or similarities affect long-term romantic relationships, Dr. Karl Pillemer found that people who are similar are much more likely to have satisfying sustained relationships. He also found that while opposites may attract, their differences make a long-term relationship substantially more difficult. According to Dr. Pillemer, opposites don't make good marriage partners.[41]

I guess we could conclude that shared values are more important than shared interests when it comes to happy long-term romantic relationships.

11. Keep Facebook and the use of other social media to a minimum! Research from the journal *Computers in Human Behavior* found that Facebook use correlated with reduced marital satisfaction and divorce rates.[42] Another study from a 2011 University of Texas at Austin survey also indicates that 32% of heavy social media users have thought seriously about leaving their spouses, versus 16% of people who don't use social networks.[43]

Why would social media be a negative influence on relationships? One theory is that networking provides instant distraction from problems that arise in long-term romantic relationships. Instead of working on the relationship, instant understanding and empathy from a stranger or someone we used to know is a click away.

I guess we could conclude that long-term relationship happiness is maintained when one focuses on the relationship instead of social media distractions.

---

[41] *See Karl Pillemer in References.*

[42] *Sebastián Valenzuela et al., "Social Network Sites, Marriage Well-Being, and Divorce: Survey and State-Level Evidence from the United States," Computers in Human Behavior 36 (2014).*

[43] *Neal Augenstein, "Study: Facebook Affects Divorce Rates, Marital Satisfaction," WTOP (July 14, 2014), http://wtop.com/news/2014/07/study-facebook-affects-divorce-rates-marital-satisfaction/.*

While there are many more components that research indicates are very important in happy long-term romantic relationships (intimacy, giving your partner space, showing each other daily physical affection, creating couple rituals, being supportive, saying "I love you" with your actions, setting goals as a couple, being willing to listen, practicing acceptance, being honest with your partner, and knowing that it is *not* the other person's job to make you happy), the elements cited above appear to be the top 11.

So now that we know the many components that make a happy relationship, let's do a survey to find out what *you* have to offer and what you might need to work on as you live life open to the possibility of finding a partner who will make a great match for you in a long-term RR.

What Do I Have to Offer?

I am usually kind to others.
☐ Yes
☐ No

I am usually kind to myself.
☐ Yes
☐ No

I am happy when others have a success.
☐ Yes
☐ No

I know what activities are fun for me and I participate in them.
☐ Yes
☐ No

I am able to express the positive emotions of:

Joy: the emotion of great delight or happiness.
I have felt joy and am able to share that feeling with others.
☐ Yes
☐ No

Gratitude: the quality of being thankful.
I am grateful for even the insignificant things in my life.
☐ Yes
☐ No

I am grateful for my experiences, whether happy or sad.
☐ Yes
☐ No

I make a practice of being thankful for my life, friends, the food on my plate, etc.
☐ Yes
☐ No

Serenity: the state of being calm or tranquil.
I make an effort to not become involved in someone else's drama.
☐ Yes
☐ No

I am aware if I have inner tranquility.
☐ Yes
☐ No

Interest: something that concerns, involves, draws the attention of or arouses the curiosity of a person.
In the past, I have had interests such as hobbies, sports, art, etc., that are outside of my romantic relationships.
☐ Yes
☐ No

Hope: the feeling of wanting something good to happen or be true.
I feel hopeful for my future.
☐ Yes
☐ No

Pride: a feeling or deep pleasure or satisfaction derived from one's own achievements and/or the achievements of those with whom one is closely associated.
I take pride in my achievements, but not in a grandiose way.
☐ Yes
☐ No

I feel pleasure when one of my friends/relatives has a success.
☐ Yes
☐ No

Amusement: the state or experience of finding something funny (not at someone else's expense).
Are you able to laugh at or find humor in various situations?
☐ Yes
☐ No

Are you able to laugh at yourself?
☐ Yes
☐ No

Inspiration: the process of being mentally stimulated to do or feel something, especially to do something creative; the excitement of the mind or emotions to a high level of feeling or activity.
Are you inspired?
☐ Yes
☐ No

Do you inspire others?
☐ Yes
☐ No

Awe: a feeling of reverential respect mixed with fear or wonder.
Are you in touch with anything that you find awe-inspiring?
☐ Yes
☐ No

Love: an intense feeling of deep affection; a feeling of deep romantic or sexual attachment to someone.
Do you feel a deep affection for others in your life?
☐ Yes
☐ No

Do you feel deep affection mainly for romantic relationships?
☐ Yes
☐ No

Empathy: the ability to understand and share the feelings of another.
Do you have the ability to sit and listen to another person and understand their feelings even though you might not agree with them?
☐ Yes
☐ No

Euphoria: a feeling or state of intense excitement, happiness, and well-being.
Are you able to feel excitement?
☐ Yes
☐ No

Are you able to feel satisfied?
☐ Yes
☐ No

Do you often have a sense of well-being?
☐ Yes
☐ No

Happiness: pleasure, joy, exhilaration, bliss, contentedness, delight, enjoyment, satisfaction.
Do you bring happiness into a relationship?
☐ Yes
☐ No

Do you enter a relationship expecting the other person to *make* you happy?
☐ Yes
☐ No

Desire: to crave or want something that brings satisfaction.
Are you able to identify what you want in a long-term romantic relationship?
☐ Yes
☐ No

I am able to enjoy sex and willing to accommodate my partner as long as that accommodation does not violate my values.
☐ Yes
☐ No

I am willing to discuss not having children.
☐ Yes
☐ No

If I and my partner decide *we* want children, I am willing to have discussions about parenting styles to determine if we are a match when it comes to the topic of raising a child.
☐ Yes
☐ No

I am willing to determine if I am financially compatible with someone I know well enough to consider him/her a PRR:
Have you spoken to your partner about finances?
☐ Yes
☐ No

     Score: Add up the "Yeses." _____
           Add up the "Nos." _____
There are 32 points possible.

If you score less than 20, you might benefit from working on developing some of these positive emotions and strengthening some of the traits that research suggests are critical in long-term happy romantic relationships. How? Start by practicing on others with whom you are not in a RR.

Some Other Characteristics Found in Happy Long-Term Romantic Relationships

People in long-term happy RRs are not *always* happy. They quarrel, slam doors, roll their eyes in frustration, sleep apart, and do many of the behaviors that are done by those in unhappy relationships. The *Huffington Post* reported that they get through "unhappy situations" by taking struggle in stride, accepting that disappointment is inevitable, putting the relationship first instead of putting the win of the disagreement first, arguing without malice, knowing how to repair a relationship bruise, and accepting that all couples have some issues that simply will never be resolved.[44]

The Quarrel and Repair Scenario

Trudy and Roland

Trudy and Roland loved each other very much. The number one thing they argued about was Roland's driving. Trudy found herself scared to death when Roland was behind the wheel. She would cover her eyes as Roland darted in and out of traffic. Roland would get angry because he felt that Trudy didn't trust his judgment when it came to driving—and he was right.

For two years, going places together with Roland in the driver's seat seeded major arguments. Roland felt Trudy was unreasonable. Trudy described Roland as "speed racer—the driver from hell." Trudy enlisted her and Roland's family to give him feedback about how they experienced riding in the car while he was driving. Roland refused to believe that others were scared and didn't want to ride with him. He appeared unable to comprehend any other perspective but his own.

Trudy had to come to terms with the fact that no matter what she said, she would not win the driving argument with Roland. She considered possible solutions and then approached Roland when she came up with what she thought was a viable solution.

TRUDY: "Roland," Trudy said as she sat down on the sofa where Roland was reading a magazine. "Do you have a moment to talk?" (It's important to get a buy-in for a conversation.)

ROLAND: "Yes," answered Roland in a disinterested manner.

TRUDY: "I've been thinking how to solve this driving issue. It is really the only thing we argue about. You know I love you and I hate fighting with you—especially about driving. It ruins our time together."

ROLAND: "I think your take on it is overexaggerated." Roland responded.

(Trudy decided not to argue this point because she had accepted that she would never win it.)

---

[44] *Winifred M. Reilly, "The Surprising Truth About What Makes Happy Couples Happy," The Huffington Post (July 5, 2014), http://www.huffingtonpost.com/winifred-m-reilly/the-surprising-truth-abou_1_b_5265073.html.*

TRUDY: "So I have a possible solution that I'd like you to consider."

ROLAND: What?

TRUDY: Well, I would be willing to do all the driving, since my driving doesn't scare you as much as yours frightens me.

ROLAND (with magazine still in hand): I'll think about it.

TRUDY: Thanks. I'm also open to another solution if you can come up with one.

Trudy left the sofa. She went outside and did some gardening she was planning on doing.

The next day, Roland told Trudy that he was willing to try her idea. Trudy gave him a big hug and kiss and told him she was very appreciative of his willingness to solve this issue between them. From then on, Trudy willingly did the driving, and during their time in the car together they talked, laughed, listened to books on tape, and generally had a good time. Did Trudy always want to drive? An emphatic "NO" is the answer. But Trudy decided she would rather drive than argue with Roland.

Trudy and Roland were able to solve this problem because they put relationship harmony before any of their individual needs to be "right." Roland's driving was a relationship issue that seemingly would never be resolved because Roland blamed Trudy's perception of his driving as the cause of the issue. Trudy came to terms that she was not going to "win" this situation by getting Roland to change his mind about how others experienced his driving skills. They both put the relationship first, and that priority enabled them to come to a creative solution.

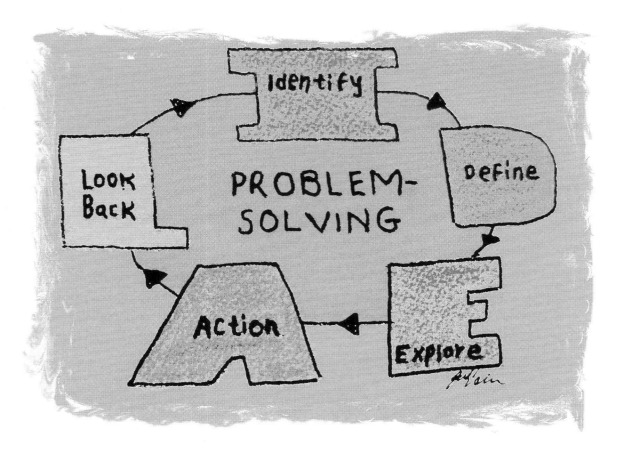

Accept that your partner is different than you are and that trying to change him/her is insulting! When one member of a couple takes on the other member as a "project" to change, that is not a relationship based on equanimity. It is a relationship that has a covert message of "I'm better than you are, and I see how you need to change to be as good as I am."

Yes, there are usually things about our partners that we might like to change, but then there are things about us that our partners would like to change too!

The "acceptance scenario" in long-term RRs:

Luca and Harriet

Luca loved fishing. Harriet loved the theater. They were in the sixth year of their marriage, and the push-and-pull in it was that Luca wanted Harriet to enjoy fishing, and Harriet wanted Luca to have a passion for live theater. Luca wanted to know why Harriet hated fishing. She had explained many times that she didn't like the outdoors, she didn't like being dirty, she thought it was a boring sport, she thought it was cruel to catch fish, and she hated campfire cooking.

Harriet couldn't understand why Luca didn't enjoy musicals like *Hamilton*. Over the years she had purchased tickets and he had grudgingly attended. He told Harriet that the seats were uncomfortable and he couldn't understand the words to the songs, "so why go and be frustrated?!"

After much discussion, Harriet and Luca decided to pursue these two interests separately. Luca joined a Meetup.com fishing group. Harriet joined a theater group. Both got their needs met. Each party treated the other with respect. They shared interests other than fishing and the theater. They did these together. They made time for separateness and for time together. They made the most of their differences by each telling the other about their fishing trip/theater production. They communicated. They accepted each other for their differences and similarities.

The uses of "thank you" and "we" turn out to be very important in long-term happy romantic relationships. Couples who said "thank you" to each other felt appreciated and had more relationship satisfaction. Couples who use the word "we" set off a program of connectedness in the brain so that instead of being in a "you vs. me" mindset, they were in a collaborative one. The use of "we" in romantic relationships was found to be a game changer in the area of relationship satisfaction.

Gil and Joanie

Gil and Joanie married after three years of dating. When I saw them, they had been married 12 years. Joanie held a prestigious position at a large corporation. As a result she was able to accumulate a large retirement account and pension. Joanie was the bread winner in the marriage. Gil held a blue-collar job that he loved, but there was no retirement or pension that came with it. They had one 10-year-old daughter, and Joanie's mother lived with them. She had provided childcare ever since their daughter was an infant. They sought my help to improve their communication.

For many years, Gil hid his hurt feelings about Joanie telling their friends about the benefits she was earning at her job. He felt like an "outsider" and a "leech" and thought that their friends believed that he had contributed no financial stability to the marriage. The truth was that Gil paid all the bills except the house payment. This enabled Joanie to contribute a large amount of her salary into a 401(k).

One night after attending a party at a friend's home, Gil voiced his reaction to the dinner table conversation:

GIL: Joanie, I felt so bad about myself at dinner.

JOANIE: Why on earth would you feel that way? I thought you were having a great time.

GIL: I felt like our friends think I don't contribute to the family. You tell them about your corporate perks, and I can't say anything because I don't have any benefits from my job. I feel like you separate yourself from me when you talk about your retirement and pension.

JOANIE: Oh, Gil. I had no idea. I am so sorry. Thank you for telling me. At the next opportunity, I will correct this.

Before we continue on with Joanie and Gil let's notice that Joanie implemented her newly learned communication skills. She did not become defensive. She listened and made a commitment to try to correct her perceived exclusion of Gil. She did not argue. In fact, she thanked Gil for telling her. Joanie's response invites candid communication. It opens the door to increased emotional intimacy. She thanked Gil for telling her his feelings instead of trying to argue why his feelings weren't valid.

The next time Joanie and Gil were at a get-together, one of their friends shared his frustration with cutbacks and compensation-reduction at his company. He told them that he had to reduce his 401(k) contributions because his family couldn't make it on his scaled-back pay. He asked Joanie if she was experiencing the same thing:

JOANIE: No, not yet. But my situation might be a little different than yours because Gil's job is what enables me to contribute so much money to our 401(k). Because of him we have been able to accumulate as much as we have.

There it was! The "thank you" for telling me and the "what we have is ours!" Be mindful that thanking your partner and using the "we" pronoun instead of "I" and "you" increases bonding and boosts partner commitment, satisfaction, and pleasure.

Intimacy is critical in happy romantic relationships. What is intimacy? It has many meanings:

In research that was conducted on 108 ethnically and religiously mixed heterosexual and same-gender relationships that had lasted for an average of 30 years, intimacy was defined as the sense that one could be open and honest in talking with a mate about personal thoughts and feelings not usually expressed in other relationships.[45]

Other research described intimacy as the process wherein an individual discloses personal information, thoughts, and feelings to a partner; receives a response from the partner; and interprets that response as understanding, validating, and caring.[46]

The dictionary defines intimacy as "close familiarity or friendship; togetherness, affinity, support, friendliness, friendship, warmth, a private cozy atmosphere."

---

[45] *Richard A. Mackey et al., "Psychological Intimacy in the Lasting Relationships of Heterosexual and Same-Gender Couples," Sex Roles: A Journal of Research 43, No. 3-4 (August 2000).*

[46] *Jean-Philippe Laurenceau et al., "Intimacy as an Interpersonal Process: The Importance of Self-Disclosure, Partner Disclosure, and Perceived Partner Responsiveness in Interpersonal Exchanges," Journal of Personality and Social Psychology 74, No. 5 (1998).*

There are different types of intimacy: physical, emotional, intellectual, experiential, and spiritual. Let's examine each of these components of intimacy so we can have a deeper understanding of their meaning.

Physical Intimacy: Of course, physical intimacy can mean sex, but it is much more than that. It includes kissing, holding hands, hugging, giving a back scratch, or putting a hand around the other person's shoulder. This physical affection releases those "feel-good" hormones, reduces blood pressure, releases stress, improves mood, and has been associated with higher relationship satisfaction.

Emotional Intimacy: Allowing yourself to be vulnerable through being honest and expressing how we feel about our fears and wants. It enables our genuine selves to be seen by our partner—imperfections and all. Emotional intimacy grows when partners share their needs and feel free to ask for what they need. Giving support by listening, stepping in to help with a task, and avoiding saying every critical thought that enters your head all serve to increase emotional intimacy.

Intellectual Intimacy: This type of intimacy is a process. It involves making plans, setting goals, budgeting, value discussions, and having a mutual understanding about these and other important issues in your life without fear of repercussion.

Experiential Intimacy: Another name for this is "recreational activity." When a couple gets involved with an activity they like to do together they are creating experiential intimacy. Playing tennis, taking a walk, or visiting an art museum, are examples of experiential intimacy. This type of intimacy also provides partners with memories of fun, which serves as a relationship bond.

Spiritual Intimacy: This is about having shared religious or spiritual beliefs and participating in some rituals about them. It can be as simple as celebrating Hanukkah, Christmas, or Ramadan, saying a prayer together, celebrating nature, etc.

Intimacy is the cement that holds long-term romantic relationships together. If there is little or no intimacy in a relationship, chances are it won't last.

CHAPTER 7

My Hopes for Every Reader of This Book

So here we are at the conclusion of this book. It seems like a lot to take in, doesn't it? Indeed, it is. Hopefully this last chapter provides you with a perspective about your past romantic relationships. I hope this new perspective will assist you in making some changes that will lead you to a fulfilling romantic partnership in the future.

The culture of romantic relationships has changed over time. The old relationship rules may not carry so much weight today. Marriage is no longer considered the only path to a staying romantic relationship. Even though the statistics don't support the concept that cohabitation leads to happier marriages, today 60% of couples cohabitate before marriage. As of 2015, 40.3% of women are having children out of wedlock. Many of us face complex coparenting challenges that provide powerful interference to maintaining a calm, romantic relationship. There are different gender roles. Same sex couples finally have found cultural legitimacy.[47]

If *you* know what your values are, changing trends need not affect you. Just because the herd does it, you need not violate your values to accommodate the larger culture. Respect your values and all the awesome components that make up your authentic self. Knowing your values and remaining true to them will greatly assist you in finding potential romantic relationships that offer possibilities for healthy long-term romantic relationships.

Be honest with yourself about what you need to change. We all have flaws. Some of them we live with. Others are of the sort that they foster unhealthy romantic relationships. Those are the ones we need to identify and rectify. I hope you find that the tools for introspection and the information about how to make yourself a great prospect for a healthy long-term romantic relationship have assisted you

---

[47] *National Center for Health Statistics (2015), https://www.cdc.gov/nchs/fastats/unmarried-childbearing.htm.*

in clarifying what you want for yourself and what you want in a romantic partner. *You don't need to "settle."*

With that in mind, I offer you a contract that you make with yourself. The one provided here is to give you an idea of how to make your own original agreements with yourself. Blank templates are on my Web page. It is my hope that the information provided in this book will help you change your romantic life for the better!

NOTE: All contracts in this book are available in electronic form to download, modify, and print.

For more information:
www.letsmakeacontract.com/contracts-rr.html

Contract with Myself

Agreement	My Responsibilities	Consequences for Breaking Agreements
I will do the Value Sort provided in Chapter 2.	Memorize my uncompromisable values and stay true to them.	Unhappy romantic relationships, suffering, depression.
I will take the quizzes provided in this book and consider my strengths and weaknesses.	Take the quizzes.	I will remain ignorant about what is getting in the way of having a happy romantic relationship.
When I find a potential RR I will learn what his/her values are and discern whether we have enough values in common.	To take the time to see if the stranger you like is the person you can love. To have compatibility discussions and not blow off things you hear that you don't like.	Repeating your old relationship cycles of meet, like, sexual intimacy, learn more about the person, argue, dislike the person, breakup, be emotionally distraught.
I will study the components of what makes a happy long-term romantic relationship and incorporate those traits into my daily life.	To know what I need to change in order to have the characteristics needed to maintain a healthy romantic relationship.	Repeated disappointment in your romantic relationships.

Appendix A: "I" Statements

"I" statements are critical in communication. They help the speaker take responsibility for his/her own feelings and needs, rather than attributing them to someone else. Any sentence that starts with "You made me . . ." assigns blame to another party and invites argument. "I" statements circumvent the "it's your fault" message and instead empowers the speaker to take ownership of feelings and opinions. "I" statements contain three components:

1. A brief, non-blaming description of the *behavior* you find unacceptable.
2. A statement about your *feelings*.
3. A very short accounting of what change you are requesting.

"When you yell at me [behavior] I feel upset and put down [feelings] because your anger reminds me of how my parents used to treat me. I'd like you to come to me when your anger passes so we can discuss what happened [offering a different method for addressing the objectionable behavior]."

I like to follow an "I" statement with the question "Are you willing to work with me on this?" If the response is "no" then the person expressing their feelings and presenting an option for change has to take the "no" as the answer and accept it, knowing that the person being addressed is not willing to work on this issue.

When using "I" statements we must be specific and avoid telling the other person what they "ought" or "should" do and avoid name calling, Resist using "I" statements that are really disguised "you" statements such as "I feel you are not being logical."

"I" statements are extremely beneficial when we must cope with "difficult" people who have a tendency to be calculating and manipulative, exploitive, overbearing, etc.

Internalize the script:
I feel _____ (name your emotions)
When _____ (name the behavior)
Because _____ (this is optional)
And I'd like/need/want _____ (name the change you are requesting)

For opioid addicts in particular, here are two "I" statements that parents have found very helpful:
"I feel angry and betrayed when you take money out of my wallet because I fear you will use it on drugs. I want you to get treatment. Are you willing to do that?"

No blame, no recriminations, no put-downs, no guilting, no demeaning, no making yourself a victim of the addict's behaviors.

A common response to this particular "I" statement is "no." Often an effective response to the "no, I will not go to treatment" is:

"I believe you. I am going to have to think about how to protect myself from your disease and I will let you know within the next three days what I come up with. I will put it in writing."

Notice there are no "you" statements, no belittling, no shaming, no accusations. End the conversation because you have said how you felt, you have made your request, you have your answer. What else is there to say? NOTHING!

When "no" is the response, create a contract. Use the templates in this book to help you.

If you practice the scripts in this appendix, over time you will have happier, healthier, and more solution-focused conversations.

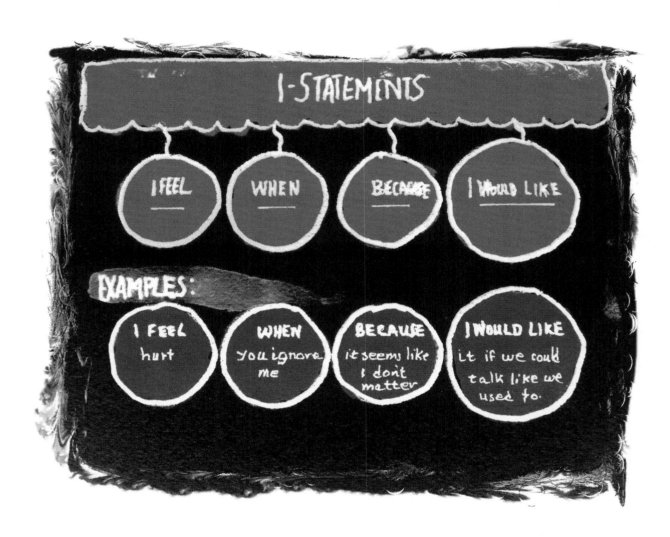

References

Adolphs, Ralph. "The Biology of Fear." *Current Biology* 23, no. 2 (2013): R79–R93.

Aron, Arthur, Christina Norman, Elaine N. Aron, and Richard E. Heyman. "Couples' Shared Participation in Novel and Arousing Activities and Experienced Relationship Quality." *Journal of Personality and Social Psychology* 78, no. 2 (March 2000): 273–84. doi:10.1037//0022-3514.78.2.273.

Atkins, David C., Donald H. Baucom, and Neil S. Jacobson. "Understanding Infidelity: Correlates in a National Random Sample." *Journal of Family Psychology* 15, no. 4 (2001): 735.

"Attention Span." Wikipedia. https://en.wikipedia.org/wiki/Attention_span.

Augenstein, Neal. "Study: Facebook Affects Divorce Rates, Marital Satisfaction." Washington's Top News. July 14, 2014. http://wtop.com/news/2014/07/study-facebook-affects-divorce-rates-marital-satisfaction/.

Banschick, Mark. "The Unhappy Marriage: Stay or Go?" *Psychology Today.* May 13, 2013. https://www.psychologytoday.com/blog/the-intelligent-divorce/201305/the-unhappy-marriage-stay-or-go.

Barnier, Amanda J., Alice C. Priddis, Jennifer M. Broekhuijse, Celia B. Harris, Rochelle E. Cox, Donna Rose Addis, Paul G. Keil, and Adam R. Congleton. "Reaping What They Sow: Benefits of Remembering Together in Intimate Couples." *Journal of Applied Research in Memory and Cognition* 3, no. 4 (2014): 261–265.

Beck, Aaron T. *Cognitive Therapy and the Emotional Disorders.* Plume, 1979.

Berg, Molly. "The Power of Thank You: UGA Research Links Gratitude to Positive Marital Outcomes." *University of Georgia Today.* October 21, 2015. http://news.uga.edu/releases/article/research-links-gratitude-positive-marital-outcomes-1015/.

"The Biggest Reasons Men Stay in Bad Relationships." eHarmony. http://www.eharmony.com/dating-advice/relationships/the-biggest-reasons-men-stay-in-bad-relationships/#.WMX2xRg-Isk.

Bingham, John, and Ashley Kirk. "Divorce Rate at Lowest Level in 40 Years after Cohabitation Revolution." *The Telegraph.* November 23, 2015. http://www.telegraph.co.uk/news/uknews/12011714/Divorce-rate-at-lowest-level-in-40-years-after-cohabitation-revolution.html.

Blanchflower, David G., and Andrew J. Oswald. "Money, Sex and Happiness: An Empirical Study." *Scandinavian Journal of Economics* 106, no. 3 (2004): 393–415. 2017. doi:10.1111/j.1467-9442.2004.00369.x.

Borchard, Therese J. "You Deplete Me: Ten Steps to End a Toxic Relationship." Psych Central. https://psychcentral.com/blog/archives/2010/03/15/you-deplete-me-10-steps-to-end-a-toxic-relationship/.

"Brain Circuitry for Positive and Negative Memories Discovered in Mice." National Institute of Mental Health. April 29, 2015. https://www.nih.gov/news-events/news-releases/brain-circuitry-positive-vs-negative-memories-discovered-mice.

Burns, David D. *Feeling Good: The New Mood Therapy.* Harper, 2008.

Clear, James. "The Akrasia Effect: Why We Don't Follow Through on What We Set Out to Do and What to Do About It." http://jamesclear.com/akrasia.

"Cohabitation vs. Marriage: How Love's Choices Shape Life Outcomes." Family Facts. 2017. http://www.familyfacts.org/briefs/9/cohabitation-vs-marriage-how-loves-choices-shape-life-outcomes.

Crawford, Colleen. "Average Time to Date before Marriage." Health Guidance. http://www.healthguidance.org/entry/15125/1/Average-Time-to-Date-Before-Marriage.html.

"Defining Your Authentic Self." Dr. Phil. July 13, 2005. http://www.drphil.com/advice/defining-your-authentic-self/.

Dyers, Ken. "Unconscious Fear." Kenja Communication. 2005. http://www.kenja.com.au/ken-dyers-203/unconscious-fear.aspx.

"Ecstasy and Oxytocin." Neuroscientifically Challenged. May 24, 2014. http://www.neuroscientificallychallenged.com/blog/2014/5/23/ecstasy-oxytocin-mdma.

Emily, S. A. "Age, Education Level, and Length of Courtship in Relation to Marital Satisfaction." PhD dissertation submitted to School of Professional Psychology. Paper 145, 2010.

Enayati, Amanda. "The Importance of Belonging." CNN. June 1, 2012. http://www.cnn.com/2012/06/01/health/enayati-importance-of-belonging/.

Finn, Karen. "Six Tough Questions You Must Ask Before Leaving Your Marriage." http://drkarenfinn.com/divorce-blog/unhappy-marriage/287-6-tough-questions-you-must-ask-before-leaving-your-marriage.

Fottrell, Quentin. "Does Facebook Break Up Marriages?" *Market Watch.* July 13, 2014. http://www.marketwatch.com/story/does-facebook-break-up-marriages-2014-07-07.

Fox, Lauren. "The Science of Cohabitation: A Step toward Marriage, Not a Rebellion." *The Atlantic.* March 20, 2014. https://www.theatlantic.com/health/archive/2014/03/the-science-of-cohabitation-a-step-toward-marriage-not-a-rebellion/284512/.

Gadoua, Susan Pease. "Contemplating Divorce." *Psychology Today.* August 2008. https://www.psychologytoday.com/blog/contemplating-divorce.

———. "How Do You Know If You Should Stay or Go." *Psychology Today.* January 9, 2011. https://www.psychologytoday.com/blog/contemplating-divorce/201101/how-do-you-know-if-you-should-stay-or-go.

Giles, Abie. "Nine Signs You Are Stuck in an Unhappy Relationship with Him." Slism. http://slism.com/girlstalk/unhappy-relationship.html.

Gordon, Lori H. "Intimacy: The Art of Relationships." *Psychology Today.* June 9, 2016. https://www.psychologytoday.com/articles/196912/intimacy-the-art-relationships.

Gottman, John. *Why Marriages Succeed or Fail: And How You Can Make Yours Last.* Simon & Schuster, 1995.

———, and Nan Silver. "What Makes Marriage Work?" *Psychology Today.* March 1, 1994. https://www.psychologytoday.com/articles/199403/what-makes-marriage-work.

Grohol, John M. "Fixing Cognitive Distortions." Psych Central. https://psychcentral.com/lib/fixing-cognitive-distortions/.

———. "Fifteen Common Cognitive Distortions." Psych Central. https://psychcentral.com/lib/15-common-cognitive-distortions/.

Hampson, Sarah. "The Secret to a Happy Marriage? Small Acts of Kindness." *The Globe and Mail.* January 8, 2012. https://www.theglobeandmail.com/life/relationships/the-secret-to-a-happy-marriage-small-acts-of-kindness/article1357638/.

Heitler, Susan. "Are You a Narcissist? Six Sure Signs of Narcissism." *Psychology Today.* October 25, 2012. https://www.psychologytoday.com/blog/resolution-not-conflict/201210/are-you-narcissist-6-sure-signs-narcissism.

Hillin, Taryn. "How Movies and TV Shows Are Changing the Way You Think about Love." The Huffington Post. June 18, 2014. http://www.huffingtonpost.com/2014/06/18/love-study-_n_5508965.html.

Hooton, Christopher. "Our Attention Span Is Now Less Than That of a Goldfish, Microsoft Study Finds." *Independent.* May 13, 2015. http://www.independent.co.uk/news/science/our-attention-span-is-now-less-than-that-of-a-goldfish-microsoft-study-finds-10247553.html.

"How to File Divorce Papers without an Attorney." Wiki How. http://www.wikihow.com/File-Divorce-Papers-Without-an-Attorney.

Jarrett, Christian. "The Science of a Happy Marriage." CNN. August 17, 2015. http://www.cnn.com/2015/08/17/health/happy-marriage-positive-emotion-science/.

Jay, Meg. "The Downside of Cohabiting Before Marriage." *The New York Times.* April 14, 2012. http://www.nytimes.com/2012/04/15/opinion/sunday/the-downside-of-cohabiting-before-marriage.html.

Jayson, Sharon. "Married Couples Who Play Together Stay Together." ABC News. July 18, 2008. http://abcnews.go.com/Health/Family/story?id=5387217&page=1.

Joelson, Richard. "Five Reasons People Stay in Unhappy Relationships." *Psychology Today.* November 8, 2016. https://www.psychologytoday.com/blog/moments-matter/201611/5-reasons-people-stay-in-unhappy-relationships.

Johnson, Matthew D. "Decades of Studies Show What Happens to Marriages after Having Kids." *Fortune.* May 8, 2016. http://fortune.com/2016/05/09/mothers-marriage-parenthood/.

Jones, Ann. "Checklist for Leaving an Abusive Husband." *Live Strong.* January 13, 2014. http://www.livestrong.com/article/218490-checklist-for-leaving-an-abusive-husband/.

"Karpman Drama Triangle." Wikipedia. https://en.wikipedia.org/wiki/Karpman_drama_triangle.

Keller, Kristine. "Limerence: When Is It More Than Heartbreak?" *Psychology Today.* September 23, 2011. https://www.psychologytoday.com/blog/the-young-and-the-restless/201109/limerence-when-is-it-more-heartbreak.

Kensinger, Elisabeth A. "What We Remember (and Forget) about Positive and Negative Experiences." *Psychological Science Agenda* 1 (2011): 1–5.

Khazan, Olga. "Divorce Proof Marriage." *The Atlantic.* October 14, 2014. https://www.theatlantic.com/health/archive/2014/10/the-divorce-proof-marriage/381401/.

Kirkpatrick, M., R. Lee, M. Wardle, S. Jacob, and H. de Wit. "Effects of MDMA and Intranasal Oxytocin on Social and Emotional Processing." *Neuropsychopharmacology* 39, no. 7 (June 2014): 1654–1663. doi: 10.1038/npp.2014.12.

Kuperberg, Arielle, and Virginia Rutter. "Cohabitation No Longer Predicts Divorce—And Possibly Never Did." Council on Contemporary Families. March 10, 2014. https://contemporaryfamilies.org/cohabitation-divorce-press-release/.

Laurenceau, Jean-Philippe, Lisa Feldman Barrett, and Paula R. Pietromonaco. "Intimacy as an Interpersonal Process: The Importance of Self-Disclosure, Partner Disclosure, and Perceived Partner Responsiveness in Interpersonal Exchanges." *Journal of Personality and Social Psychology* 74, no. 5 (1998): 1238.

LeDoux, Joseph. "The Emotional Brain, Fear, and the Amygdala." *Cellular and Molecular Neurobiology* 23, no. 4-5 (2003): 727–738.

"Limerence." Wikipedia. https://en.wikipedia.org/wiki/Limerence.

Love, Tiffany M. "Oxytocin, Motivation and the Role of Dopamine." *Pharmacology, Biochemistry and Behavior* 119 (April 2014): 4-60. https://www.ncbi.nlm.nih.gov/pubmed/23850525.

Mackey, Richard A., Matthew A. Diemer, and Bernard A. O'Brien. "Psychological Intimacy in the Lasting Relationships of Heterosexual and Same-Gender Couples." *Sex Roles* 43, no. 3 (2000): 201–227.

Mann, Denise. "How to Break Up Gracefully." WebMD. http://www.webmd.com/sex-relationships/features/how-break-up-gracefully.

"Marriage and Divorce." American Psychological Association. www.apa.org/topics/divorce/.

Martin, Lauren. "Seven Stupid Reasons People Stay In Relationships When They're Unhappy." *Elite Daily.* September 29, 2014. http://elitedaily.com/dating/reasons-people-stay-in-relationships-when-unhappy/776627/.

"Mirror Neurons." Brain Facts. November 16, 2008. http://www.brainfacts.org/brain-basics/neuroanatomy/articles/2008/mirror-neurons/.

Muise, Amy, et al. "Sexual Frequency Predicts Greater Well-Being, But More Is Not Always Better." *Social Psychological and Personality Science.* November 2015. doi: 10.1177/1948550615616462,

Navarra, Bob. "Three Research-Based Tips for a Happy & Healthy Relationship." The Gottman Institute. February 11, 2015. https://www.gottman.com/blog/3-research-based-tips-for-a-happy-and-healthy-relationship/.

Obringer, Lee Ann. "How Love Works." How Stuff Works. February 12, 2005. http://people.howstuffworks.com/love.htm.

Olson, Randal S. "144 Years of Marriage and Divorce in One Chart." June 15, 2015. http://www.randalolson.com/2015/06/15/144-years-of-marriage-and-divorce-in-1-chart/.

Osborn, Kimberley A. "Marriages Resulting From Short-Term Premarital Relationships: Are They Successful?" *Academia.* December 12, 2011. http://www.academia.edu/2912278/Marriages_Resulting_From_Short-Term_Premarital_Relationships_Are_They_Successful.

Palitz, Jeff. "Should I Stay in My Marriage for the Kids?" *Parents.* http://www.parents.com/advice/parenting/relationships/should-i-stay-in-my-marriage-for-the-kids/.

Parker-Pope, Tara. "Sex and the Long-Term Relationship." *The New York Times.* March 22, 2011. https://well.blogs.nytimes.com/2011/03/22/sex-and-the-long-term-relationship/.

"Partners in Parenting." The Center for Parenting Education. http://centerforparentingeducation.org/library-of-articles/focus-parents/partners-parenting-working-together-team/.

Pawelski, Suzann P. "The Happy Couple." *Scientific American.* https://www.scientificamerican.com/article/the-happy-couple-2012-10-23/.

Penny, Brian. "Seven Signs You're Truly Unhappy in Your Relationship." Life Hack. http://www.lifehack.org/articles/communication/7-signs-youre-truly-unhappy-your-relationship.html.

Pillay, Srini. "How Is Unconscious Fear Affecting You?" Leading Brains. March 30, 2010. http://andyhabermacher.blogspot.com/2010/03/how-is-unconscious-fear-affecting-you.html.

Pillemer, Karl A. "'Opposites Attract' or 'Birds of a Feather'—What's Best for a Long Marriage?" The Huffington Post. April 2, 2013. http://www.huffingtonpost.com/karl-a-pillemer-phd/marriage-counseling-opposites-attract_b_2557391.html.

———. *Thirty Lessons for Loving: Advice from the Wisest Americans on Love, Relationships, and Marriage.* Avery, 2015.

Reid, Diana. "Three Easy Steps to Becoming Your Authentic Self." Life Hack. http://www.lifehack.org/articles/communication/3-easy-steps-becoming-your-authentic-self.html.

Reilly, Winifred M. "The Surprising Truth about What Makes Happy Couples Happy." The Huffington Post. May 5, 2014. http://www.huffingtonpost.com/winifred-m-reilly/the-surprising-truth-abou_1_b_5265073.html.

Rosenberg, Marshall B. *Nonviolent Communication: A Language of Compassion.* Puddledancer Press, 1999.

Sack, David. "Limerence and the Biochemical Roots of Love Addiction." The Huffington Post. June 28, 2012. http://www.huffingtonpost.com/david-sack-md/limerence_b_1627089.html.

Sarkis, Stephanie. "Seven Keys to a Healthy and Happy Relationship." *Psychology Today.* January 2, 2012. https://www.psychologytoday.com/blog/here-there-and-everywhere/201201/7-keys-healthy-and-happy-relationship.

Schramm, David G., James P. Marshall, V. W. Harris, and Anne George. "Marriage in Utah: 2003 Baseline Statewide Survey on Marriage and Divorce." Salt Lake City: Utah Department of Workforce Services. 2003.

Springer, Shauna H. "Key Factors That Impact Your Odds of Marital Success." *Psychology Today.* June 30, 2012. https://www.psychologytoday.com/blog/the-joint-adventures-well-educated-couples/201206/key-factors-impact-your-odds-marital-success.

Stanley, Scott M. "The Hidden Risk of Cohabitation." *Psychology Today.* July 20, 2014. https://www.psychologytoday.com/blog/sliding-vs-deciding/201407/the-hidden-risk-cohabitation.

Stritof, Sheri. "Cohabitation Facts and Statistics You Need to Know." *The Spruce.* March 21, 2016. https://www.thespruce.com/cohabitation-facts-and-statistics-2302236.

Taibbi, Robert. "The Art of Solving Relationship Problems." *Psychology Today.* January 17, 2011. https://www.psychologytoday.com/blog/fixing-families/201101/the-art-solving-relationship-problems.

Tartakovsky, Margarita. "Accessing Your Authentic Self." Psych Central. https://psychcentral.com/blog/archives/2011/01/04/accessing-your-authentic-self/.

Teachman, Jay. "Premarital Sex, Premarital Cohabitation, and the Risk of Subsequent Marital Dissolution among Women." *Journal of Marriage and Family* 65 (May 2003): 444-455. http://www.jstor.org/stable/3600089.

Tennov, Dorothy. *Love and Limerence: The Experience of Being in Love.* Scarborough House, 1999.

Thomas, Caitlin. "Five Facts About Cohabitation You May Not Know." The Daily Signal. February 13, 2015. http://dailysignal.com/2015/02/13/5-facts-cohabitation-may-not-know/.

Tugend, Alina. "Praise Is Fleeting, but Brickbats We Recall." *The New York Times.* March 23, 2012. https://mobile.nytimes.com/2012/03/24/your-money/why-people-remember-negative-events-more-than-positive-ones.html.

"Unmarried Childbearing." National Center for Health Statistics. https://www.cdc.gov/nchs/fastats/unmarried-childbearing.htm.

Valenzuela, Sebastián, Namsu Park, and Kerk F. Kee. "Is There Social Capital in a Social Network Site?: Facebook Use and College Students' Life Satisfaction, Trust, and Participation." *Journal of Computer-Mediated Communication* 14, no. 4 (2009): 875–901.

Walsh, Susan. "Everything You Always Wanted to Know About Infidelity but Were Afraid to Ask." Hooking Up Smart. July 24, 2013. http://www.hookingupsmart.com/2013/07/24/relationshipstrategies/the-definitive-survey-of-infidelity-in-marriage-and-relationships/.

Washburn, Carolyn, and Darlene Christensen. "Financial Harmony: A Key Component of Successful Marriage Relationship." The Forum for Family and Consumer Issues. https://ncsu.edu/ffci/publications/2008/v13-n1-2008-spring/Washburn-Christensen.php.

Watson, Leon. "Humans Have Shorter Attention Span Than Goldfish, Thanks to Smartphones." *The Telegraph.* May 15, 2015. http://www.telegraph.co.uk/science/2016/03/12/humans-have-shorter-attention-span-than-goldfish-thanks-to-smart/.

Whitbourne, Susan Krauss. "The Twelve Ties that Bind Long-Term Relationships." *Psychology Today.* June 5, 2012. https://www.psychologytoday.com/blog/fulfillment-any-age/201206/the-12-ties-bind-long-term-relationships.

Wong, Brittany. "The Top Ten Reasons People Stay in Unhappy Marriages." The Huffington Post. December 15, 2014. http://www.huffingtonpost.com/2014/12/15/why-people-stay-in-unhappy-marriages_n_6330292.html.

Acknowledgments

None of my books would have ever been published without the dedicated, kind, patient, supportive dream team of my illustrator, Jack Varonin; graphic designer, Casey Brodhead, PsyD; editor, Mark Burstein; Gail Kearns, my publicist who has been such a help and support; Kathy Moran, my web designer has been unbelievably creative in designing a unique and user friendly site; and publisher, Andrew Benzie. Honestly, I am just the scribe, but you six are the creators, the people who have made my writings come alive. I shall always be so humbly grateful for your expertise, confidence in our product, hard work, availability, advice, and feedback. If my "thank yous" were all placed in a bucket and each were worth a dollar, it would be equivalent to paying off the national debt!

About the Author

Dr. Ann Schiebert has vast experience with teens, adults, and families in the area of chemical dependence, codependency, dual diagnosis, and trauma. She has spent years designing ways in which families and couples can have a more harmonious relationship based on making agreements with each other. Dr. Schiebert also teaches couple's communication and codependency recovery classes. The communication "scripts" that her patients learn have been time tested and have assisted them in alleviating interaction styles that create contention.

In addition to her work at the Walnut Creek, California, mental health clinic of a major national HMO, Dr. Schiebert works in its emergency department and hospital as a psychiatric crisis specialist. She also has a private practice that specializes in codependency issues. This is the third volume of her *Let's Make a Contract* tetralogy: *Getting Your Teen Through Substance Abuse* and *Getting Your Teen Through High School and Beyond* were published in 2016.

Dr. Schiebert is the mother of three adult children and lives with her partner, Tom Rohrer, PhD, in Lafayette, California.